Happy to be

Different

Personal and Money Success Through Better Thinking

Dan Danford, CFP®

Author of *Stuck in the Middle*

First Edition Design Publishing

Sarasota, Florida USA

ISBN 978-1506-909-46-2 HCJ
ISBN 978-1506-909-47-9 PBK
ISBN 978-1506-909-48-6 EBK

LCCN 2020916666

August 2020

Published and Distributed by
First Edition Design Publishing, Inc.
P.O. Box 17646, Sarasota, FL 34276-3217
www.firsteditiondesignpublishing.com

Many of these columns have previously appeared in the *Kansas City Star*, *Investopedia*, or the *Business Journal Leadership Trust*. Danford has also written for *Financial Planning Magazine*, the *NAPFA Advisor*, *Morningstar*, *Advisor Perspectives*, *Medical Economics*, and *Research*. He has been quoted or featured in the *Wall Street Journal*, *Kiplinger's Personal Finance*, *New York Times*, and the *Chicago Tribune*, among others. This and his other books are available on Amazon.

Contents

A Note from the Author

Success with money is mostly different than portrayed. Most people I know with money are thoughtful, hardworking, and happy. They enjoy a robust family life and find time to do the things they love. Money is a helpful tool, not a vengeful master.

My first day in the money business was April 1st, 1984. I started as a trust officer for First National Bank in St. Joseph, Missouri. It was an unlikely place to land given my prior work selling supplies and furniture for an office design firm.

But I'd recently graduated with an MBA and I applied to all the local firms who might need someone with advanced schooling in business. It was a very short list in St. Joseph, and I was lucky that someone at the bank knew my father. I got hired to help the trust department administer and market tax-qualified retirement plans.

Despite my lack of experience in that realm, I did pretty well. I was smart enough and ambitious. I picked it up quickly – even the massive rule changes that defined that era in retirement planning. But none of those things were all that special. A lot of industry professionals were learning and adjusting to a changing environment.

No, what made me different was my ability to explain; I was really good at explaining things to clients, their employees, and people in our community and bank. This was the secret seed that grew into my career.

As this seed grew, I was invited to explain things in a variety of publications. Early on, most articles or columns were for trade journals and industry media. I was also invited to speak at meetings and events and on radio and television. I did an ongoing opinion series for one local television station and became a resource for news organizations.

This book, though, grows from a different branch on that same tree. The articles I wrote for ordinary people became my obsession. Why? It is because the mass of information created for ordinary people isn't very helpful. It's boring. It's hard to understand. It's dictatorial. It's irrelevant. Did I mention that it's boring?

So, I created a different style of writing about money to answer these problems. I tried to explain things in a way that makes sense to normal folks. I dispensed with the bossy junk, the worn-out examples, and the rules of thumb routinely ignored by millions. Instead, I tried to make the lessons real and explain things in a way that normal people can understand.

I also argue against the austere budget dictated by finance professionals everywhere. Have some fun, I say. Go ahead and drink that latte. Order those season tickets. Let eBay or Amazon help you succeed. Buy the house you want and don't fret much about payments.

So, I'm happy to be different. This is a collection of some favorites. Most have already appeared elsewhere and were written and published for the general public. You might note that a few lean towards business or helping employees succeed because that's another target for my same message.

Also, my recommendation is that you find a good advisor to help you with money. The chapters explain why. But that doesn't mean it's the only route to success and happiness. Many people love personal finance and investing, and they do a fine job. As you'll see, my experiences show that a lot of people could do better with some good help.

I hope you'll see that success with money doesn't need to be boring.

Dan

Part 1

Happier Ways to Think About Money

GO AHEAD AND DRINK THAT LATTE

One of the toughest aspects of personal finance is balancing longer-term goals against the realities of today. Many finance writers and advisors prescribe an austere daily budget or worse as the foundation for success.

That prescription is so common that it has become cliché. Do a quick finance search on-line for Starbucks or pizza or even daily lunch options and you'll find dozens of stories explaining how that expense can be transformed into your retirement nest egg. The math is simple: three dollars a day times 200 workdays per year times twenty years invested in a good growth fund at eight percent equals $29,654 (!). Wow think what you could do with that!

(Except in twenty years, that same three-dollar cup of coffee will probably cost closer to six. God knows about the price of other stuff.)

It's magic ... and dumb. These types of simplistic illustrations do more harm than good. Most people aren't going to skip their daily Starbucks or weekly pizza or brown bag it every day for lunch. Behavioral evidence is abundant. At this moment in this culture, that is not the way to achieve financial success. It's a Don Quixote-like railing at cultural windmills.

I absolutely reject the notion that personal finance has to be boring. In fact, one reason people fail is because they envision it as boring, and it very likely has been drudgery most of their lives. A good chunk of personal failure can probably be traced back to some Ben Stein sound-a-like high school teacher droning on about coffee and pizza and Taco Bell.

Here's a better approach. Find a way to do the things you like. You like cars? Well, cars are expensive, but a lot of people drive very cool cars. How do they afford them? What kinds of careers and decisions allow them to drive the car of your dreams? What will it take to put you in that same driver's seat?

You like going to ball games? Season tickets are high, but the stadiums are full every single game. How is it that thousands of people have money enough to sit in those seats every time the whistle blows? What are they doing that allows them this luxury that you'd enjoy so much?

One time, I was startled when a good friend chided me for leaving a nice tip at a restaurant. He pointedly remarked, "you must be rolling in cash." Nope. But here's the truth. If you make the right big decisions, the little ones don't matter so much.

If you make the right big decisions, the little ones don't matter so much. I have a good job. I live in a nice neighborhood in a house I bought for a reasonable price. I do a bit of consumer research before spending money. I send money to my company retirement plan with every paycheck and I make sure my investments are reasonable and diversified. I rely on quality advisors to help me succeed.

Maybe some of those things are kind of boring, I don't know. Here's what I do know, though. I can afford a latte if I want, and pizza, too. I can go to ball games and drive the current car of my dreams. I enjoy eating in nice restaurants and do so as often as time allows.

And I can afford to tip the hard-working wait staff. It's not because I'm rolling in cash. It's a little thing, I know, but I can afford it because I do the right big things.

HOW YOU SPEND IS MORE IMPORTANT THAN HOW YOU BUDGET

If you pressed me to guess, I'd say that spending decisions are the most important factors in financial success. No matter your income, no matter your tastes, no matter your sense of discipline or frugality, the ways you spend money will determine success or failure.

Some finance writers and advisors prescribe an austere monthly budget as foundational for success. But that idea of saving/ budgeting has almost become cliché. Do a quick Google search for Starbucks or pizza or even lunch options and you'll find dozens of stories explaining how daily savings can be compounded into a retirement nest egg. The math is simple: three dollars a day times 200 workdays per year times twenty years invested in a good growth fund at eight percent equals $29,654 (!). Wow - think what you could do with that! (Except in twenty years, that same cup of coffee will probably cost six dollars. God knows about the price of other stuff.)

Those numbers are like magic ... and so dumb. These simplistic budget illustrations do more harm than good. Most people aren't going to skip their daily coffee or weekly pizza or brown bag lunch every day. Behavioral evidence is abundant. At this moment in this culture, that is not the likeliest way to achieve financial success. It's a Don Quixote-like railing at cultural windmills.

I absolutely reject the notion that deprivation is necessary. In fact, one reason people fail is because they envision personal finance as boring, and it very likely has been drudgery most of their lives. A good chunk of personal failure can probably be traced back to some Ben Stein sound-a-like high school teacher droning on about coffee and pizza and lunches.

It's all about balance and thoughtfulness. One of the toughest aspects of personal finance is balancing longer-term goals against the realities of today. A budget by itself isn't a lot of help with smart spending decisions. You don't have to give up everything you love.

If you make the right big decisions, the little ones don't matter so much. In his books, *The Millionaire Next Door* and *The Millionaire Mind,* Dr. Tom Stanley revealed that millionaires tend to make purchases with a practiced eye for the future. They buy top-quality merchandise based on the *lifetime* costs of ownership. Quality shoes or furniture may cost more up front but last longer and deliver better performance. The wealthy tend to purchase based on *value instead of price.*

A former colleague repeatedly focused on price instead of value. We were on the same purchase cycle with new automobiles. I'd choose a Honda or Jeep based on research and an eye towards resale value. Ignoring this methodical approach, he instead opted for the "cheapest" deal. Surprisingly, we often spent similar amounts.

But every three years when it came time to trade, I *always* got more money for my car — sometimes a lot more — and he never understood why. He would blindly launch right back into his "buy the cheapest" cycle. An otherwise bright fellow, he was living proof that destructive spending habits are not confined to the uneducated.

An affluent client once explained to me how driving a Mercedes-Benz was less expensive than driving a Chevy or Ford. He reasoned that operating costs and depreciation were less than with cheaper cars. I didn't do the math, but I do know that Mercedes-Benz autos have great resale value, which means lower annual depreciation. The up-front cost is markedly higher, but once you make the purchase, those numbers might make total sense.

In fact, most consumer goods retain little liquidation value. If you want to estimate the value of an item, ask yourself what a sensible person would pay for it on eBay or Craigslist. If you owe a large balance on a big-ticket item — such as being "upside down" on an auto loan — it can be extremely difficult to unload without suffering a significant loss. The liquidation price for vehicles is called resale value. In real estate, it's called market price.

By itself, price is a dubious measure. Many items — especially new consumer goods — reflect costs of production and marketing rather than inherent value. The price of a new television or trendy headphones is based on manufacturing, transportation, advertising, and competition. The resulting price may or may not represent value.

Before buying anything, gauge the product's price as a used item. Stripped of the "commercial" costs, the item's true value is revealed. For products with inherent or collectible value, the used price might be close to the new price; for most others, the new price is an expensive trap. Beware of falling into price traps, especially with borrowed money.

Truly, spending decisions are more important than budgeting. *If you make the right big decisions, the little ones don't matter so much.*

BLOW IT, MOW IT, AND GROW IT: TAX REFUNDS AND OTHER WINDFALLS

There are a lot of ways to get money, but surprises are the best. There's almost nothing better than a surprise gift or unexpected bonus. Sometimes a tax refund or inheritance might be larger than expected. Maybe a long-shot lottery ticket or game show winnings can add some welcome heft to your wallet or purse. No matter the source, extra money is a welcome guest in any family home.

If you are the fortunate beneficiary of a tax or other windfall, I suggest that the money should satisfy your basic human instincts as well as accomplish some good. I believe people do best when they splurge a little and save a little. I suggest three destinations for the money:

Blow it. This is the fun part — the splurge. Take a weekend vacation or even a cruise if that appeals to you. Using some of the money to pursue pleasure is a piece of the American Dream ... and the memories will bring you joy for years to come. We all need some joy in our lives. A lot of financial plans fail because they ignore the need for joy. Where's the joy in receiving a tax refund or bonus if it all goes toward paying off the credit cards or replacing the furnace?

Mow it. Think of this as financial lawn maintenance. If you have a leaky roof, debts to pay, or need to establish a fund for emergencies, use some of the money to address issues that are holding you back. Enroll in a class if you suck at budgeting; order some software to track expenses or balance your checkbook. Few people succeed financially without occasionally mowing or maintaining their financial lawn.

Grow it. An obvious choice is to reroute a chunk of the money into your retirement account or college funds. For maximum growth, plant seeds that can prosper over a decade or two. Jim Stowers, founder of the American Century family of mutual funds, once noted that the "perfect time to plant an oak tree is twenty years ago. The next perfect time is today."

But financial growth isn't the only option. In fact, it may not even be the best option. Perhaps a few college classes or a new certification at work might boost your career. A time management consultant could help you carve that essential chunk of space into your week to start that book you've been pondering. A public speaking coach could inject some bells and whistles into your business presentations. Personal growth often offers a faster and healthier return than financial investments. Hey, learning to play the guitar might be a lot of fun! (And spur creativity in other areas of your life you didn't know you had).

Personal growth is a powerful use for money. Books, lessons, seminars, and experiences all bring lasting value for the dollars spent. Some of that value might translate into increased earnings or lower expenses; some might add substance to life or lead to better use of precious resources. In almost every case, the value created exceeds the money spent.

I reject the notion that personal finance has to be boring. In fact, one reason many people fail is because they envision it as boring, and it very likely has been drudgery most of their lives. So, the remedy to the boredom challenge is to add some spice toward accomplishing goals.

No disrespect for the boring stuff, which has been well-documented when it comes to personal finance. Every bookstore and library are crammed with "how to" financial books. Countless internet sites offer advice. Much of it is relevant and helpful, but knowing something isn't the same as doing it. That's where most people come up short.

For windfalls, blow it, mow it, and grow it. And this year, look at money, both the expected kind and the unexpected kind, as genuine freedom, and a path toward getting "unstuck." You'll be surprised by the differences a thought shift will make.

LET EBAY HELP YOU DECIDE

A family statement of net worth (balance sheet) is a powerful financial tool. A statement is easy to compute, updated quickly, and offers a great way to evaluate decisions.

First, to build your family's statement, start by listing the honest resale value of all things you own. List all houses, cars, boats, household goods, collectibles, and anything else of value (probably higher than you think, but lower than you'd like). Next, add financial assets. Include bank, brokerage, or mutual fund accounts. Include IRA accounts or retirement plans from work. Include the cash surrender value of insurance policies. In short, this list should include everything you own with the current value.

The second half is - hopefully - a much shorter list. Here, list everything you owe with today's payoff value. Start with the mortgage. Then, add any car, student, or consumer loans. List the balances on credit cards or money you owe family members. Don't forget loans on insurance policies or money owed to a company retirement plan.

Simply, Family Net Worth (FNW) is the difference between what you own and what you owe. It's the liquidation value of your financial life. If you sold and liquidated everything you own and paid off all debts, what would be left in your wallet?

Knowing this number helps you financially. It's a running tally of financial progress. Update the numbers occasionally and see if your FNW is rising or falling. A rising number indicates progress; one that slips requires attention. (Of course, there are life stages where FNW is expected to fall - college years for children is one.)

It's also a spectacular decision-making tool. Say, you're trying to decide whether to replace a car or start a mutual fund account. Consider what will happen to your FNW five years from now. Estimate the future worth of the car and the mutual fund five years from now. Does this help decide? Similar processes can help decide between two cars (which will have better resale value?) and houses (ditto).

I suggest to clients that they employ what I call the eBay

test before reaching significant buying decisions. Simply, go to eBay and look for the item you are considering. Most consumer items can be entered in the Search bar and an entire list will pop up. Use the exact item number from the manufacturer and you'll likely find new, used, and refurbished versions. For this purpose, we're interested in the value of the used item.

Why? Because once you buy, the used value is what goes on the asset side of your FNW. What happens to your FNW when you take out $500 from the bank to buy a new camera? You took $500 of cash and swapped it for $200 of used camera. Nothing wrong with that, but your FNW would stay higher if you'd purchased the camera used from eBay! A refurbished item falls somewhere in between and often features a warranty just like new; the best of both worlds?

The eBay test helped you reach an informed decision. Family Net Worth was a helpful measurement tool.

Not every family decision is reached based on finance. But finance should be considered as part of any major decision. Understanding FNW helps all of us make better choices.

A Fresh Idea About Your Stale Mortgage

What if you could pay 2009 prices in 2019? You could buy a 1st class stamp for $.42, a gallon of milk for $2.69, or a pound of your favorite bacon for $3.19. You could see the latest movie for $7.25 or buy a carton of Coke for $6.

Almost everyone has (or had) a mortgage, but mortgages are often portrayed as a sort of necessary evil ... you need one to buy a house, but you should pay it off as fast as you can.

My take is different. You'll need to understand monetary inflation to learn this lesson. You've seen inflation, we all have, but it's unlikely you've given it much thought.

The price of milk or bacon goes up a few cents each year; that's inflation. We grow used to these modest price changes. We expect prices to go up and we expect our pay to rise, too. Mostly, these small increments aren't dramatic, and we don't fret much about them. Price increases are built into the economic system.

You've watched inflation all your life, but you've mainly seen it in reverse. Although rising prices are what we see, what is really happening is that the purchasing power of the United States dollar is falling slightly. Tomorrow's dollar is worth less than todays. Look at it in this way: would you rather have what a thousand dollars bought in 2009 or today?

Most times, these price increases (or decreases in the dollar's value, depending on which way you look at it) are small. The U.S. Federal Reserve Board sets their inflation target at 2% each year, although some years are a bit higher and others a bit lower. A few times – the 1980s, for example – were a lot higher for a lot longer. But, for purposes of this explanation, that merely strengthens my point.

Back in 2009, I bought a house. The price was $180,000. Now the usual process of buying/borrowing requires a 20% down payment, so we're going to talk about a $150,000 mortgage. But I tricked the system. Instead of paying $150,000 with those valuable dollars then, I deferred part of the payments until today. I'm paying these with today's dollars – worth some 18% less today than they were in 2009.

Think about this. Today's entire payment was locked-in using those old dollars. Every payment I will make is with less valuable dollars. Take $150,000 and divide by 360. That makes average principal payments of $416.66 per month for thirty years … except those last monthly payments will be worth half as much (buying power) as earlier ones. In other words, I tricked the system big time.

Wait, wait, wait, you say. That example doesn't include interest. Right. Interest is a big part of mortgages payments. In fact, at todays' rates, the actual monthly payment (principal and interest only) for the $150,000 mortgage would be $733.53. Interest alone adds $114,069.27 if I keep the house and make all 360 monthly payments. That's a lot of money.

But, still … even those last interest payments will be made with much-diminished dollars. Anyone with longer-term mortgage payments will affirm that monthly payments that seemed high in past decades look ridiculously low compared to the new neighbor next door. In other words, thirty years hence, my entire payment is being made with cheap dollars.

And – this is key – while payments are made with old dollars, the house's market price continually adjusts to new dollars. No one will care what I paid for the house in 2009. In 2039, the price will be determined by the value of other houses of that future era. If we assume the same 2% inflation rate, the old dollars will be worth half as much (.54) as when purchased (old dollars), but the house will be worth almost twice (1.81) as much (new dollars).

I will have paid $264,069.27 (plus the $30,000 down payment) for a house now worth $325,800. Of course, this assumes the value of that particular house appreciates at the same pace as inflation. If it's in a good neighborhood or housing in general appreciates at a higher rate, I'll have done even better. If housing values grow annually by 2.57% (the national average from 1989-2019), the house will be worth $385,374.

So, here's my point. Don't worry so much about paying off your mortgage. Don't worry so much about the interest you'll pay. Chances are good that interest costs will be offset by inflation, and then some. Instead of worrying about the mortgage, focus on building emergency reserves and your 401(k) retirement account. If you still have extra money, start an investment account using solid growth mutual funds.

Let the mortgage and inflation work for you as the house price rises and you enjoy that "locked-in" payment from yesteryear!

WHY AREN'T ALL SMART PEOPLE RICH?

It's an intriguing question. It makes sense to believe that superior cognitive skills would be transferrable. It makes sense that traits measured on a standardized IQ test would help anyone be a better truck driver, bank teller, or computer programmer.

If you've ever taken an IQ test, you can see why. Standard questions try to uncover how quickly you spot patterns or solve problems.

What's the next number in this sequence? 2, 4, 8, 16, ___

      A.   32 B. 35 C. 36 D. 39

Now smart people aren't better than anyone else. But, quickly seeing patterns can lead to accurate medical diagnoses, strong business opportunities, and solutions for tough problems.

The ability to spot patterns, remember numbers, reason, and solve problems is an advantage. Generally (I repeat, generally, we all know exceptions), the smartest truck driver will be better than the dullest. The smartest bank teller will be tops in the bank. The smartest computer programmer, well, he or she may write the next Windows program or create the next Google.

Some jobs are known for attracting bright people. Again, generally, most would agree that doctors are smart and so are lawyers. We'd agree that university faculty members or

16

engineers have good brains. Maybe the top minds in Silicon Valley or Wall Street fit this profile, too.

Logic suggests that those smart professions thrive in finance, too. Certainly, Wall Street bankers and Silicon Valley moguls are among the richest people in America. Doctors and lawyers tend to earn well. University professors and engineers earn above-average wages, too.

That isn't the whole story, though. High annual income isn't the same as being rich. Some professions tend to pay better than others, but that doesn't assure financial success. Many people with lavish lifestyles never accumulate wealth … the trappings cost too much. At year-end, they have little with lasting value to show for all they spent.

What I have observed by watching bright people.

Being smart isn't a big bonus for investing. If you are blessed with extra smarts, you probably rely on them for everything. You can find the fastest route to the office in the morning or estimate in your head how long the trip to grandma's will take. You may organize things well or fix the office printer better than anyone else. Being smart carries over into many areas; *thinking that investing is one of them could lead you astray.*

Investing is counter-intuitive. That's one reason many people fail. Sometimes, things that seem right turn out to be wrong (buying into a sizzling market or selling when things seems gloomiest). Other times, simple luck can be extremely profitable.

Investing can be especially confounding for smart people. The patterns you see probably don't really exist, and influential factors for the markets are too numerous to comprehend. The markets truly are a living organism (millions of emotional people) responding to brand new circumstances every single minute. They adapt to changes instantly.

There may be a few savants who can master the markets. There may be people or groups who devise winning ways to capture market inefficiencies for a while. There are certainly some people with very long streaks of very good luck. It's a mistake to count on any of these.

Some tips to avoid the smartness trap.

Being smart doesn't have to be a handicap. Here are some suggestions to counter the magnetic pull of cognitive strength:

- Avoid bad information – A lot of investment information is created as a sales tool. The story behind Snapchat or Facebook was written to pique your intellect and interest. The risks don't get the same attention. Good decisions using bad information don't work.

- Don't trust the wrong people – Where do you get information? Where do they get information? Are they truly helping you understand or selling some product?

- Allow time to do it right – Smart people are very busy. If you are distracted, you are too busy to invest right. One mark of cognitive skills is speed. It won't help you here.

- Don't trust assumptions based on your own experience – Most investors know just one set of circumstances (their own) and one period of history. It may be a decade or longer, but it is still just one longish episode. Lessons may not be universal or typical.

- Favorite projects require caution – Everyone has hobbies and interests, and those might offer some advantage; if you are a computer geek, for instance, you may pick and follow technology stocks. How does that help with international stocks or government bonds? A well-rounded portfolio is crucial in controlling risk. Concentrating on favorites is not a complete strategy.

- Read the fine print – Too many investment risks aren't obvious until disaster happens. Without help, people are awful at understanding and mitigating risks. If some investment offers high returns, the risk is there even if you don't sense it.

- Ruthlessly evaluate results – What would you say to an advisor who bought the wrong thing? What would you say to an advisor who didn't protect you from risks? What would you say to an advisor who missed a 30% upward market swing? Well, those same issues hurt even if you did them to yourself.

I'm a professional cynic. I bring a skeptical eye to everything I do, especially for my clients. But even professional investors must trust others. I have sources of information and people I trust because history tells me they are trustworthy. No one does successful investing completely on their own.

I'll add another telling point. Many smart people choose vocations or professions with low financial rewards. Teachers and preachers both fit this model and I've seen first-hand examples of really smart people earning relatively low paychecks. I guess we'd say that money isn't the main motivator in their lives.

For the record, that is a hallmark of many of the most successful people I know. Money isn't the main motivator in their lives. Financial success is a by-product of careful, deliberate, choices.

5 HABITS OF FINANCIALLY SUCCESSFUL PEOPLE

There are a lot of good ways to measure success, and my favorite definition rises from personal or family goals. To me, success is awareness of specific goals and deliberate action toward those goals. There are often distinct financial steps along the way and the attainment of each step is reason to celebrate. And, of course, most successful people create new goals as they finish the old ones!

Your measures of success likely differ from mine. That's fine. However, you define success, these are some common traits I see among the most successful people I know:

1. *They spend time with other successful people.*
   Warren Buffett and Bill Gates are fast friends.
   That's not a coincidence. Whether it's through
   church or community clubs or work groups or
   neighborhood fellowship, "nothing succeeds

like success" (a quote from my father Thad Danford). People tend to gather based on common values and goals, and good friends inspire each other. My observation is that people of similar values often share similar life goals.

2. ***They accomplish things today, but big decisions are based on future goals.*** One of my observations is that little things don't matter so much if you get the big things right. I read one article that suggested 80% of our work time is wasted. I'd be slightly more diplomatic and suggest that just 20% of our efforts are spent wisely. But if you spend that 20% right – moving towards your stated goals – the other 80% may not be that important anyway.

Those home budgeting articles often criticize a weekly pizza or daily latte at Starbucks. That costs you "HUNDREDS OF DOLLARS EACH YEAR," and it has to be a "STUPID WASTE OF MONEY." Yeah, that's exactly why people ignore those articles … the truth is that a family with solid education, an emergency savings account, and contributing regularly towards the 401(k) can blow a few bucks on pizza or coffee. Seriously, lighten up, people.

3. ***They set their own agenda.*** Many working people exercise little control over daily tasks and activities. Yet, many of their bosses left dreary jobs because they wanted more control over both personal productivity and income. I've seen the same thing among nonprofit executives and educators. The most successful people jump towards responsibility and control. More control at work means more control in life.

    Sadly, I think a lot of people live life like the shiny metal ball in an old pinball machine; they bounce from one painful obstacle to the next. Everyone faces obstacles, but most successful people don't let obstacles knock them off course. They keep working towards those goals, even when someone throws a hurdle in the way. Sometimes they use that hurdle as a ladder up to their next goal!

4. ***They spend wisely.*** You'd expect this from a money guy, but spending cash is only part of the challenge. Successful people recognize how *all* resources add to or detract from goals. This

includes time, continuing education, relationships, and – predictably - money. I often tell students that they won't be able to start their own business at age 40 (see # 3 above) unless they make careful preparations along the way. If your personal goal is to hike around the world, you'll need time, money, and smarts to make that happen. Maybe you can find a good friend who shares that goal and will happily join in the preparations.

5. ***They see retirement as another stage of the success process.*** The happiest and most successful people I know are still working. Many of them retired from the formal workplace, but they stay active in a variety of worthy pursuits. They work for the United Way or help with their grandson's Boy Scout troop or teach Sunday school every weekend. (You have to admire President Jimmy Carter teaching in his nineties, and as he endured chemo treatments for cancer.)

Nothing drives home the success point quite like this: happy, vital, productive people keep moving towards thoughtful and meaningful goals. Even as they check things off their list, they replenish the supply to keep moving forward. Maybe those "stretch" goals are the genuine key to success.

FORBES 400 OFFERS INSPIRATION FOR ALL

The NFL has 32 teams. Each team has an active roster of 53 men. That's a few shy of 1,700 players worldwide. The rosters change each and every week due to injuries, roster moves, and other adjustments.

The Forbes 400 is even more exclusive than the NFL, although similar in some respects. Each year, Forbes compiles this list of 400 wealthiest Americans. There are a lot of familiar names on the list, with some moving up, some moving down, and others dropping off the list completely.

We are talking the top one percent of the One Percent here. Officially, there are 3.2 million Americans in the wealthiest One Percent. This Forbes list is the top 400 of those folks. Most of us can't even imagine this kind of wealth, let alone entertain hopes of achieving it. Still, it makes fascinating reading if nothing else.

This year, it took a net worth of $2 billion to make the list although the average among this tiny group is almost $7 billion. Among first timers on the list (there are 22), most are entrepreneurs (19). Some 169 people in America have net worth over $1 billion and *still didn't make this list.* That's billion with a B ... they are millionaires a thousand times over and still can't make this exclusive list!

What can we learn from this year's edition? Are there specific lessons for the rest of us? A couple of things. First, none of these people work for the man. America is the land of opportunity and the quickest way to the top is to start a successful business ... or be born to someone who did. People on this list are not typical wage-earners.

Also, many of these fortunes are powerfully-tied to the U.S. stock market. Not in the same way as you or me (through our 401k plan or brokerage accounts), but the wealth they create is primarily in the corporate stock of a company they founded. Jeff Bezos, Bill Gates, and Mark Zuckerberg aren't rich from trading stocks. They are rich because the corporations they started – Amazon, Microsoft, Facebook - have immense value for millions of shareholders. As stock prices rise, so do their personal fortunes.

That brings another important point. To earn a billion dollars at anything takes scale. Not skill, scale. A store-front enterprise in Saint Joseph, Missouri is unlikely to ever serve enough people to produce this kind of wealth. America has 325 million people, and the world around 7 billion. Incredible wealth requires a big chunk of them as customers. It's no mistake that Amazon, Microsoft, and Facebook founders make this list. They serve millions of customers every hour of every day.

We can still learn from them. Most of us won't start an international company and we'll never enjoy the type of fame that earns a nickel each from millions of fans (Oprah Winfrey or Mark Cuban, for instance). Our opportunities are much more modest. Even so, we can build our work lives around helping others in a mutually-beneficial way.

If our opportunities are modest, so are our needs. Truthfully, no one needs a billion dollars. My guess is that most of the Forbes people are both surprised and dismayed by their success. Many of them, including Bill Gates and Warren Buffett, have pledged to give most of their money away to charity when they are done. They didn't expect it, they don't need it, and they won't pass it along to family or friends. In other words, money isn't the main point to their lives.

That's likely the most powerful lesson for you and me, too. We don't need to make this annual list to be successful or good. These people are extraordinary in almost every way. Their ideas, talents, work ethic, ambition, and outsized opportunity earned them a spot on the most exclusive of exclusive lists. Congratulations to them, and I pray they use that wealth to accomplish great things.

For us, the scale is smaller, but our tools are exactly the same. Ideas, talents, work ethic, ambition, and opportunity can create remarkable success in any endeavor. We - not the famous guy at #248 on this list - will make America great!

CHOICE IS THE FINEST LUXURY OF WEALTH

When someone mentions wealth, I'll bet your mind goes to a few luxury brands like Mercedes Benz or Rolex. Perhaps your mind's eye wanders to exotic vacations on the water in Europe or Hawaii. Maybe you fantasize a Learjet jaunt to visit a distant friend.

Those are all good, and worthy of mention. But none of them matches choice – more options - as the finest luxury of all. It's not so much that you will buy a Mercedes Benz, but that you can if you want! Or a Cadillac, BMW, or Porsche for that matter.

Lack of choice is the opposite extreme.

I note the vehicles around me as I drive to work each day. There are nice cars, but the ones that make me smile are the junkers. I'm not smiling in laughter; I'm smiling in recollection of earlier days on our journey. Junk cars weren't ever my goal, but they were our reality in days before choice.

In fact, cars provide a great lesson. Everyone needs a car. Car choices are endless - but they are not endless for everyone. On the socioeconomic ladder, choices expand with each rung to the top. Those junkers? Mostly driven by people with little money, poor jobs, and bad credit. Their car options are mostly limited to cash or "no credit check" dealers charging ridiculous interest rates.

As you step up a rung, more choices open before you. You might buy a good used car or an inexpensive new one. Now the car dealer can help with financing and so will your banker. You'll be able to choose from a larger palette of automobiles, but also compare interest rates and payment terms (3-year, 4-year, or more). Don't like that price from one dealer? Cross the street to find another.

If nothing else, cars can offer some helpful lessons about credit and borrowing:

- Some things are best bought with cash money or checks. Groceries, rents, utilities, and entertainment items all into this category. The need for ready cash limits some of your choices.

- Credit cards can be helpful for convenience, and even for short-term loans. Maybe the washing machine died, or you need a new suit for a job interview. Use the card and pay it off quickly. Even credit cards offer better terms and rates as your wealth grows.

- As your situation improves, so does your ability to borrow. But the ability to borrow doesn't guarantee quality choices. Maybe your circumstances allow a

$20,000 loan ... is it better to buy a used Chevy or a new Kia?

Good borrowing is a choice, too.

Now a brief explanation. In business school, they teach that borrowed money can often be used to make more money. It's called leverage, and some things we buy hold future value better than others. Borrowing to buy something that holds value is always better than borrowing for something that doesn't.

Also, buying decent cars and houses provide collateral to your lender. Because of this, interest rates are lower than other loans. You've earned better choices!

- This helps answer the question about that used Chevy or new Kia? The right answer is which one has more value after the loan is paid off.

- This also helps explain why mortgages are wealth builders. Houses tend to rise in value, so a loan to buy one often produces long-term positive results.

Borrow to take a step up.

One last concept. Education is a good choice to move up the rungs. It's maybe not a sure thing, but it likely works better and faster than other options. Unfortunately, education costs money and a lack of money is one thing you're trying to fix. Borrowing for school can help (and is probably worth it), but there are some ideas to enhance your success:

- Choose a field and degree that pays well. It's dumb to borrow a lot of money and earn a degree without commercial value. Use your electives to study the fun stuff.

- Find a respected community or state college and enroll there. I promise it will be meaningful and it will cost a fraction of the prestige party schools.

- Get involved with internships, practice-ums, and experiential learning. Potential employers love people with experience, no matter how small. And many full-time staffers started as interns.

Smart borrowing can be a solid financial tool.

Borrowing is unique among financial tools. In a way, it is different from budgeting or coupon clipping or depriving yourself of things you want. No, experience teaches me that success comes from making good decisions. And, oddly enough, better buying and borrowing choices become available with every move up the ladder.

And the fruits of all those good choices? Yes, you guessed it. The finest luxury of all. More choices.

SEED MONEY OR MAD MONEY?

I was enjoying a chat with one of my best buddies last weekend. Like they often do, the conversation wormed its way around to retirement and finance. One of the sincere things he said perked my attention.

"I guess what I'd really like is to finance my retirement and then, when I'm done, pass along a bit of seed money for my son."

Earlier, he'd mentioned that he forecasts retirement out to age 98 for himself as a sort of insurance that he won't run out of money. We use similar figures in our professional financial projections for clients; it's not that everyone makes it that far, but a significant portion of retirees do. One recent tally showed over 70,000 hundred-year-olds among our population.

"You do realize," I prompted him, "that Tyler could be an old man before he inherits that seed money." We chuckled, but it wasn't all that funny. It was a moment of insight with dramatic consequences. Adult children today face a different financial path than ever before.

Seed money is a great idea. The notion rises out of our agricultural past. It's the little bit today that grows into eventual prosperity. It is applicable to almost anything: crops, inventory, education, investments, or (even) relationships. Put value into them today and they grow into something much more valuable over time.

But time is the key variable. Crops won't grow in a week. Seed money for college is better spent early when lessons will be planted into a career that might blossom throughout adulthood. Inventory for a brand-new retail store takes a thousand turnovers to become a successful chain. Modest annual contributions can grow into a sizable retirement fund, but only if they compound across several decades.

So, this is my blinding insight. Meaningful contributions may require a different approach than you already think. It's not bad to leave a nice bequest (everyone loves extra money!), but similar amounts at age 35 can be far more impactful than at age 70. Will it be seed money or mad money?

Here are some terrific ideas I've used with my own family or seen among my successful clients:

- Buy education for grandchildren so adult children can focus on retirement compounding.

- Buy inspiring vacations for the entire family. Everybody wins when grand-parents create powerful memories. Without help, vacations are a luxury that many families miss.

- Loan money to children for sensible purposes. Your portfolio probably contains bonds (loans) to government entities and corporations. You can add a loan or two to family without hurting investment performance. (Treat it like a genuine loan, though, with documentation and payment schedules.)

- Invest in family businesses. Every business needs capital. Your loan or investment in a family business helps both you and your family. Again, treat this like any other investment. Consult your lawyer.

- Invest in continuing education. A college education today gets stale faster than any other time in history. People need to update skills and knowledge ... both for work and personal satisfaction. You can help them grow and prosper throughout their lives.

This brave new world offers both challenges and opportunities. Most people tend to see the challenges instead of the opportunities. However, the rewards for some adjusted thinking can be rich.

Leaving something after you are gone will be welcome, no doubt. Helping before you are gone, though, might be more inspiring and productive. Further, watching your family prosper – through education or some other helpful resources – can be a priceless experience. Why wait until you are dead to help?

FOR LAWNS OR MONEY, PROS ADD VALUE

The rich get richer. The poor get poorer. And the green get greener.

Although there are many ways to care for your lawn, the two primary ways offer a helpful illustration. And, of course, neither of these approaches touch on the default option which is just do nothing; let it go to weeds, mow occasionally, never trim and never water. A lot of people apparently choose default with a capital D.

But if you want a lawn to look nice and enhance the value of your home, you can do-it-yourself or you can hire a lawn service. Either approach can create stunning results, but that's where the similarities end.

Many do-it-yourselfers enjoy the process. They spend hours happily working in the yard and own necessary tools and supplies. At the least, they own a mower, trimmer, blower, spreader, and either hoses or an irrigation system. They maintain a sizable supply of fertilizer, weed control, and grass seeds. They create and maintain a schedule for organic applications and – of course – mowing. Spring months, especially, may require several clippings per week. Nutrients are likely required 3-5 times each year. There are a lot of moving parts.

A lawn service, by contrast, requires less personal attention. They just show up when something needs doing and they take care of it. They own and maintain the equipment, provide supplies, and hire the required labor.

Now, the do-it-yourselfer may argue that he or she is saving money, but I doubt it. Many cost comparisons fall short because some costs aren't included ... if you truly calculate the initial investment in equipment, annual wear and tear as you use it, continuing costs for replenishing supplies, and the value of labor you yourself provide, you'd have a much stronger comparison.

My guess is that these are closer than you think. A commercial lawn service probably costs the same or less if genuine numbers are analyzed across all those areas. After all, they are buying supplies in bulk and using industrial equipment with longer lives and less maintenance. That equipment is likely more efficient than we'd buy at home, too.

They also hire strong young people to do the work, too, which means they are doing it better and faster than I ever could! By other objective measures, all else about the lawn service *may be better*, too. They work with hundreds of lawns and have experience with a wide variety of landscape challenges. They routinely sharpen the mower blades and your busy schedule at work won't cause a delay in applying fertilizer or mowing the lawn. Because of their equipment and expertise, the quality of work is often better than most do-it-yourselfers can achieve.

The investment business offers important parallels. There are tiers of options lying between do-it-yourself and full discretionary investment management services. But the lesson is still the same. You can spend the time, buy and perform research, create and implement a strategy. Or you can hire professionals that spend their entire work lives doing those same things. Additionally, they'll bring insights and economies of scale that you can't match. It's pretty hard to argue against these points.

Honestly, you can keep doing-it-yourself and you'll probably do a decent job. Or you can default and just let luck determine your financial outcomes. But neither of those two choices offer the best value. Many investors would be far ahead to let professionals do their heavy lifting. A green thumb - as in lawns or money - grows ever greener with quality professional help.

Part 2

STAY HAPPY BY

LEARNING MORE

CONQUERING RISK INTOLERANCE IS ONE KEY TO SUCCESS

I once read a book once where economist Ben Stein labeled "risk tolerance" as "institutionalized malpractice." Before you get too excited, let me explain what I think he meant because I think it is really quite important.

My experience (not formal research) suggests that people are naturally risk-adverse. Risk tolerance starts low, and rises over time with experience, education, cultural norms, and success. It also cycles up or down with specific circumstances, the economic climate, or a wider variety of other factors. But, generally, people prefer less risk over more risk in investing.

This creates a very real dilemma. Risk free investments aren't adequate to meet most people's financial goals. Simply, most people don't earn enough to accumulate sufficient amounts for their retirement needs. In today's world, retirement years can easily last as long as working years.

So, for most people, setting money aside each month is insufficient. Funding a reasonable retirement *requires* riskier assets, compounding over several decades. Nearly everyone's preference would be less-risky investments (risk intolerance); everyone's need is for more-risky investments (risk tolerance).

The notion of risk tolerance is that each person has a different ability to withstand portfolio fluctuations. Based on that personal ability, the perfect portfolio would be one that maximizes performance without exceeding the fluctuation limit. And, also based on that ability, there's no point in pursuing a more aggressive portfolio posture.

I get all that, but I'm uneasy with the implications. One major implication is that millions of people are destined to fail financially (as measured by their ability to fund a decent retirement) because they can't withstand portfolio fluctuations! It's like a built-in excuse to fail.

How would we respond to these similar statements? "Well, I'd rather not get polio, but I hate big needles and I can't tolerate inoculations." "Sure, I understand the principle behind insurance, but I can't afford to insure my car." "I'd like to quit smoking, but I just can't stop." "I know I shouldn't be on the phone during church, but what if I miss a call?" Seriously.

How are any of those different than, "When I retire, I'd like to have some extra money set aside, but I just can't stand any risk. I keep all my money in the bank." It is mostly the same argument, but money makes it a very different measure. And this is the powerfully important point: what is the personal and family cost for tolerating that apprehension? Simply, it means failure to achieve what you'd like for retirement.

If any of this sounds like you, what needs to be done to overcome that anxiety? Are there steps you can take to become more risk tolerant? Here are a few suggestions from me:

- **Learn more.** Most studies on this subject suggest that risk tolerance rises as people learn more about investing. Find a good book or some articles on investment basics. Investing isn't hard but understanding 4-5 solid principles is enough to help.

- **Start small**. Similarly, people tend to become more risk tolerance with investment experience. Stock market cycles can be scary at first, but they become easier after you've survived one or two. If you start with smaller amounts, the first cycles won't seem so bad, either.

- **Create separate wallets**. Set up accounts for different purposes. Money being saved for a new car shouldn't be mixed with money for the kids' college. A retirement account should be separate, too. This can help because the longer-term money (retirement accounts) feels less urgent than the car money … allowing you a bit more comfort and tolerance.

- **Ignore CNBC**. Any of the television news or other outlets benefit from drama. This is entertainment first, and education second. Every story feels important because anxiety is a key part of drama (horror movies, anyone?). If you are already nervous, this is a recipe for failure.

Investing isn't rocket science, and almost anyone can learn enough to succeed. But our natural risk intolerance is a huge impediment. Anyone wanting to achieve long-term financial goals needs to fight back. Don't let risk intolerance conquer your ambition.

RECIPE FOR SUCCESS: MODERN PORTFOLIO THEORY

Have you ever tasted vanilla extract? Do you eat raw eggs? Do you bake? Though vanilla extract and raw eggs aren't pleasing to the palate, they are ingredients for a world-class cake. When combined with flour, sugar, and other staples, and heated in the oven, they turn into a mouthwatering bite of feathery goodness. Somehow, the combination is better than any of them on their own.

Portfolios are just like that. Some of the ingredients (stocks, bonds, or mutual funds) might not be appealing on their own. Individually, they might be too risky or too obscure, or too concentrated for a direct holding. But, as part of a diversified portfolio, they add an element that makes for solid long-term performance.

We hear good questions all the time.

> *"Why keep so much money in bonds when they are paying such a low rate?"*

> *"I just watched Cramer on CNBC and he said that small companies are going to underperform this year. Let's get rid of them."*

Most of the time our answer is this: they are part of your portfolio because the combined ingredients are better than any of them would be individually.

Up until the 1950s, most investment research focused on individual stocks and bonds. Which is the best stock – Ford or General Motors? How do you decide between several corporate bonds? What methods of choosing predict the best purchase for a portfolio?

In 1952, the *Journal of Finance* published Harry Markowitz's pivotal paper "Portfolio Selection." (Harry Markowitz, "Portfolio Selection," *The Journal of Finance*, Mar 1952, Vol. 7, No. 1.) Over the next forty years, considerable academic research studied portfolio behavior.

In 1990, three people — Markowitz, Merton Miller, and William Sharpe — earned the Nobel Prize in Economics for their portfolio studies. That body of knowledge came to be known as Modern Portfolio Theory. It's tested and true and stands as genuine investment science today. Like any science, the total body of knowledge continues to grow over time.

The key concepts regard diversification. Diversification wasn't a new idea in investing. But some diversification findings rocked the investment world. First, it's important to remember that risk and reward are completely and totally related. That's the one absolute economic truth. It's always been understood that riskier investments reward investors with higher returns. That's why, over the long haul, stocks tend to outperform bonds. Higher performance is pay for taking higher risks.

[Note: In investment research, portfolio fluctuation is used as the primary measure of risk. Dramatic portfolio fluctuations are more likely to produce a negative outcome.]

What wasn't widely known before Modern Portfolio Theory is that mixing and matching investments can positively alter a portfolio's risk/reward profile. In fact, the most stunning finding was that mixing certain types of investments can *lower portfolio risk while increasing portfolio returns!*

Let that sink in.

A common truth that is that all investors seek high returns with low risk. It's part of human nature. Most of us are born with extreme risk aversion; "I want something that pays high returns without any risk."

Now, after sixty-some years of academic testing, we discover (they discovered; we just follow their work) that the right mix of investments can reduce portfolio fluctuations without hurting returns. Or, at least, returns aren't reduced to the degree you might expect.

Think about two stacks of paper. One holds ten thousand dollars' worth of stocks, the other ten thousand dollars' worth of Treasury bonds. The expected ten-year return from these stacks is quite different and somewhat predictable. Without quibbling over details, let's agree that the stock stack should grow at an estimated ten percent rate annually, the bond stack at five percent.

For sake of example, let's assign a simple risk number to each. Let's pretend that our scale rates the stocks with a risk of two and the bonds with a risk of one.

Now, if we mix the two stacks to form a portfolio, we'd expect that the expected annual return would be seven-point five percent (7.5%), halfway between the two. Our expected risk should be one point five (1.5, again halfway between the two).

What the research discovered, however, is that the returns are above *7.5%* and risk *below 1.5*! Stocks and bonds meld together to increase returns while lowering risks. Clearly, the combined portfolio is better than the sum of the parts. This was a revolutionary investment idea.

Further, this magic works with any "dissimilar" assets. Mathematically, dissimilar assets are any investments with negative coefficients of correlation. The simple way to explain this is that one zigs while the other zags. So, you can increase portfolio returns and reduce risks by matching real estate with stocks. Or bonds. Or precious metals. The more diverse a portfolio, the more dramatic the improvement.

Though this improvement is counterintuitive, it's been proven again and again. You can improve a conservative portfolio (raise returns and reduce fluctuations) *by adding some riskier holdings!*

According to Modern Portfolio Theory, a portfolio mix of eighty-five percent bonds and fifteen percent stocks is safer and more productive than a portfolio of one hundred percent bonds! Believe me, before Modern Portfolio Theory, no one would have believed this! Some people still have trouble believing it.

There's at least one important disclaimer to this. Though the science is real, it's somewhat inexact. It's a bedrock concept for *long-term investing*. It doesn't have predictive power; in fact, it argues against trying to predict the future. Rather, it suggests that a properly constructed portfolio will perform better with less risk over a wide variety of market cycles.

It's a bit like predicting the weather. The science is helpful over time, but it fails to be accurate with all forecasts all the time. Modern Portfolio Theory doesn't even try to forecast the future; diversified investors are rewarded with higher returns and lower risks across many market environments. There will be rough spots, but – relatively, takings both risks and rewards into account – a Modern Portfolio should outperform others.

RED SNAPPER HELPS UNDERSTAND PORTFOLIOS

You need fish. For the sake of illustration, let's pretend you own a seafood restaurant and you need fresh fish every single day. In a sense, your business – your very livelihood – depends on the fisherman's ability to catch fish daily in the varieties and quantities you need.

Now, nothing can be easier or cheaper than using just one fisherman. He ventures out each morning, returns around noon, and you meet him at the dock when he arrives. The fish are fresh and his schedule predictable. Besides that, Mr. Fisherman is delighted to sign a contract giving you preferred pricing.

There's only one small catch (you've already spotted it, haven't you?). Sometimes the fish don't bite. Mr. Fisherman meets you at the dock with an empty creel. Franticly, you race from boat to boat to boat seeking tonight's red snapper. Too late, you discover that today's bay is empty. The fish moved on during the night. Perhaps tomorrow will be better.

Tomorrow? What about today? There's an anniversary party ... and a business meeting ... lunch customers already waiting ... well, you get the picture. Tomorrow is too late, and crisis is a bad time to learn anything.

Looking back, one lesson is very clear. You can't rely on one fisherman or just one bay. Instead, you need several (maybe dozens) of fisherman working with a variety of bays, baits, and boats. Good fisherman, all, but each subject to the ocean's movement and whims. When one fails, another succeeds. Through variety, you develop a reliable source of fish for your restaurant. And, a safety net for your livelihood.

Mutual funds and investment managers are a lot like those fishermen. By design, they use certain techniques in certain waters. They are experts at catching fish, but only when fish in their part of the bay are biting. Otherwise, they troll for the day when fish return. That's their job and any of them do it rather well.

A lot of investors stumble over this idea. They can't understand why you'd stick with an investment or fund without stellar recent performance. They see international investments or small company stocks, for instance, and assume you should ditch them from the portfolio. Lately, we've heard rumblings about bonds and bond funds.

But you shouldn't blame the fisherman when fish aren't biting. That's like blaming the farmer for bad weather or an airline pilot for turbulence. Most of us do the best we can with the circumstances we encounter. Some are good, others are bad. But that doesn't make us good or bad! In investing, circumstances tend to cycle between good and bad, but the goods tend to outweigh the bads over time.

Diversification is important because it offers an element of safety to portfolios and that is why we do it. Significantly, we also know that Modern Portfolio Theory bolsters that concept by showing how mindful diversification increases returns and reduces volatility (risk). In other words, variety adds both safety and quality to investment portfolios.

All those different investments provide insurance. The past year or years haven't always been good to each of them, but their day will come. And when it does, some other investment sector will likely fall off. In this sense, diversification protects us from a fishless day. Something is biting somewhere, and we want to assure that we are there for it.

BETTER CHOICES FOR INVESTING TODAY

The investment business used to be conducted through distinct product silos. Brokers or insurance agents were aligned with companies that created financial products. Those products were exclusive to each shop. The shop down the road might have a similar product but it would necessarily differ in some ways. The broker or agent was paid to sell house products.

You can see where this was flawed. I faced the same dilemma when I bought a new car. At a critical point, I discovered that I liked the car a lot, but not the dealership. I had to choose: give up the car or buy from a dealer I didn't trust or like. Other people faced the opposite problem. They like a particular dealership but aren't happy with available brand names or models. They'd prefer a different car, but they want to buy it through their chosen dealer.

With cars, maybe you'd rely on a salesperson to answer technical questions, arrange test-drives, and help with financing. You trust them to help you reach the right decision, sign necessary papers, and – hopefully – you go home happy.

What if you learned afterward that the salesperson earned special incentives all along the way? That the car you bought paid higher sales commissions (and cost more) than others? That your lender awarded glamour vacations to sellers closing the most "deals?" Ultimately, you overpaid for the car and missed better financing opportunities. Would this upset you? Of course, it would.

This was even worse for investment clients. The opportunity lost from excessive fees or higher prices compounds over time. Ultimately, your retirement or college accounts were considerably smaller due to the imposed costs.

There are two big challenges with this traditional model for investing. First, each company silo limited the choices available to clients. It they only offered their own brand of products, that excludes hundreds of similar products offered through other channels. Obviously, some of those house products might be pretty good, but others are likely average or worse.

Secondly, salespeople might be manipulated through the compensation system. Certain products might offer higher incentives, encouraging additional attention. In fact, from a management perspective, that's exactly why special incentives are offered. Good for the company, good for the salesperson, probably less-good for the client ...

In the car business, a solution might be a car supermarket – featuring multiple product lines through a single dealer. You could get any vehicle you want through the same local dealership. Salespeople would be salaried, or at least they'd disclose how they are paid on every car. Then, you could reach truly informed decisions.

A similar approach for the investment business would be a platform offering multiple competing products with a neutral fee structure. This way, a client could approach with certain questions or needs, and an advisor could answer with genuine knowledge and flexibility. Every option could be considered and nearly every situation satisfied. No worries about hazardous incentives or false claims. Ongoing relationships could be built around mutually beneficial service.

Today, thousands of independent advisors have adopted this precise approach to serving clients. They typically use third-party (no financial ties) investment platforms created by Schwab, Fidelity, or TD-Ameritrade as a source of products and services. They charge fees based on the services provided, but in some neutral fashion; either a flat fee, retainer, or percentage of portfolios managed are typical. Some charge hourly or project fees if they are more practical.

An independent investment advisor may be the right solution for your situation. A Registered Investment Advisor (RIA) is regulated by the United States Securities and Exchange Commission or your state securities regulator.

Both are governed by the federal Investment Advisor Act of 1940.

Traditional brokers and other firms are also better today than before. Some have improved their product offerings and pay schemes. Any improvement is welcome, but the improvements aren't universal. Make sure the firm and professional you choose is one of the good ones. Check out their disciplinary history on the FINRA website.

The old silo system was the problem. Behavior was motivated by the products they sold, and the way people were paid. For the consumer, it was a dangerous system. Much better options are available today.

DO NOT TAKE A KNEE IN RETIREMENT

Volume is one advantage that professional advisors enjoy. I encounter people every day who have experience and opinions about finance and investing. Some of them are as knowledgeable about stocks, bonds, and economics as members of my own professional team.

What they lack, though, is a broader perspective. They've read articles, studied their budgets, browsed the internet, talked with a few friends and family. All good, but sort of isolated in a small bubble of similar situations, time horizons, and ideas. If most your knowledge base comes from these past ten years, that's a serious limitation on your ability.

A seasoned professional is one way to combat that. Simply, any advisor worth consulting has worked with hundreds of clients, diverse needs, and widely-varied economic climates. No guarantees, but the perspective offered is necessarily broader than your own.

There's one old (powerful) idea that helps makes this point. It's very common to hear that you should reduce or eliminate portfolio risk as you near retirement or when your portfolio is large enough to meet your needs. Or, as they say in football, take a knee when you've already won the game. This idea sounds great and, since many people are risk-adverse anyway, it encourages them to do what they already want.

But it might not be what is best. I don't recommend that anyone liquidate a long-term portfolio and take a knee. My recommendation would be to reduce risk assets, perhaps, but maintain a modest portion as an inflation hedge and for a few other reasons. Many advisors recommend 25-35 percent in longer-term (5+ years) portfolios. Liquidity needs and potential taxes must be considered, too.

That very common idea of eliminating risk requires more thought today.

The first point I'd make is that portfolio time horizons often run longer than people predict. So, the guy contemplating retirement at age 60 might assume that his $1 million IRA is sufficient to fund retirement. He's likely not thinking that he'll need income for 30+ years. Keep it in a conservative, balanced portfolio and he might draw an inflation-indexed $40,000 per year for life. Shift it to bank certificates or money market funds and he'll gradually lose ground from year-to-year. The problem is less severe for someone at age 80, but it could still be a factor over another 15 years.

Another point is that market risks are less than they seem for periods longer than 5 years. While anything might happen during the next 5 years, the 5-year investment outcome is more predictable than people think. So, most times, people with 5+ years in their investment horizon will do better than they fear. Importantly, many people at age 80 or 85 still have a time horizon of 5+ years.

Third, even a small amount of portfolio "risk" adds significant compound returns. It's one thing to say, "we don't need any more money," but possibly another to deprive others. Heirs, charities, and other causes will gladly accept more when that day comes. Another way of saying this is that those parties might receive a gift diminished by inflation if you are too conservative with investing.

Comfort is important in retirement and portfolios should be tuned to your targeted risk level.

Yet, too little risk can be as damaging as too much. With longer lives, broader perspective, and better understanding, many old ideas require new attention. The notion of eliminating portfolio risks in retirement sounds good, feels good, and may garner praise from some of your friends and family. My considerable seasoning says to give this idea a bit more thought.

This isn't meant to disparage the fundamental idea of adjusting risk in your golden years. These are nuances to be considered as you think about retirement investing. And they are likely nuances that rise from outside your personal knowledge bubble.

FOUR FOUNDATIONS FOR A SOLID RETIREMENT

It's easy to get lost in details. If you've ever built a house, you know first-hand how taxing it can be. Hundreds of niggling details command astounding amounts of time. Lights, appliances, carpets and floor coverings, finishes … the decision list can be exhausting.

Planning retirement can feel a bit like that. But, like building a solid house, the bigger things matter most. You can easily adjust colors or fixtures in the future. The right foundation creates lasting value.

These are four foundations to a solid retirement.

Income: Everyone needs income. For most retired folks, that comes from a combination of Social Security and personal savings. Some groups also enjoy old-style pensions, but those are rarer and rarer. Teachers, railroad workers, and many government employees (local, state, and federal) have pension benefits.

The key to income success is coordinating monthly expenses with monthly income. In many homes, personal savings includes both pre- and post-tax dollars (more on this in a minute). Choosing a withdrawal scheme to minimize taxes can make a big difference, as can the ability to adjust for changing circumstances.

Two non-traditional products are increasingly popular. Deferred annuities can be used to ensure future income. A single premium today will promise regular income for later years, after, say, 85 or 90 years old. With one of these specialized insurance products, you won't outlive your money.

Reverse mortgages can also be used to supplement income. Scrutiny has squeezed many of the costs and disadvantages from these loans, and they can be successfully used to tap home equity for better purposes. I'd still be wary of aggressive sales techniques; approach your regular mortgage professional for help.

Retirement Plan Distributions: Although pensions are less common, other types of retirement plans are plentiful. Profit sharing, 401(k) plans, Tax Sheltered Annuities (453 plans), Deferred Compensation (457 plans), and Individual Retirement Accounts (IRAs) abound. Additionally, both Simplified Employee Pensions (SEP) and SIMPLE (Savings Incentive Tax Plan for Employees) plans are IRA-based retirement plans.

Most plans provide a single large retirement payment that requires special consideration. First, the typical distribution may be larger than any other financial transaction. It's a daunting amount for many retirees. Second, any portion not rolled into an IRA-Rollover account faces both federal and state income taxes. Third, various IRA-Rollover alternatives can impose high fees, investment restrictions, and/or surrender charges.

Some employers allow retirees to remain in an employer plan. If plan fees are low and there are sufficient good investment options, this can be a good choice for savvy investors. However, other people could benefit from professional help and broader choices.

Larger distribution amounts and less-sophisticated investors gain the most from professional assistance.

Investing: The old retirement investing rules don't apply any more. People live decades in retirement and being too conservative is every bit as perilous as being too risky.

I suggest that people look back to 1988. How much was a new car then? How much for rent or house payment? How much for a month of groceries? What do those things cost today? What will they cost in 2048? Because people retiring today face a 30-year retirement horizon.

If retirees invest a new car's worth of money today, we need for it to still buy a new car in 2038 or 2048. That's the new investment challenge. Simply, conservative investing – bonds, bank certificates, fixed annuities – probably won't keep pace with the rising price of groceries or automobiles.

A long-term diversified portfolio of blue chip stocks and bonds offers the best chance of keeping up. If you can't do that on your own, seek a quality professional to help.

Estate Planning: Everyone knows you should have basic estate planning documents – a will, powers of attorney, and maybe transfer on death ownership for bank accounts or real estate. But beneficiary designations are often overlooked and critically important today.

IRA-Rollover and other retirement accounts and insurance policies transfer according to the most recent designation of beneficiary. There is no joint ownership and a will or trust won't matter. Plus, IRA-Rollover and annuity accounts can impose sizable tax liability to the beneficiaries. Not designating a beneficiary creates an estate issue and prompts accelerated taxable distribution from IRA or annuity accounts.

Make deliberate choices about who gets what, and how. Proper estate planning can minimize taxes and maximize gifts to family or charity. Take the time to get this right.

Foundational Lessons:

Flexibility: With today's long retirement time horizon, it's a genuine mistake to restrict flexibility. Products that impose sizable surrender charges or lock in serial payments are problematic. Circumstances change and you'll want to change with them.

Consolidate: Many of us have far too many accounts. There are old 401(k) accounts for jobs we left years ago. There are bank deposits and accounts where we used to live, and on-line accounts that seemed like a good idea back when. This creates an absurd amount of paperwork and coordination.

Eliminate small holdings: It can be fun to own shares of Disney, Harley Davidson, or Facebook. For most of us, those holdings are tiny relative to our overall portfolio. Fun, but unproductive and inefficient. Time to simplify life and get serious.

Volume pricing: Smaller accounts pay higher fees. It must be that way for brokers, agents, and advisors to help people starting out. But everything from mutual funds to insurance policies impose lower fees on larger buyers. Seek an advisor or firm with large portfolio expertise.

Hire a professional: Some people are suspicious about hiring a professional, and that's likely because they've suffered a bad experience or two. The world has changed, though, and genuine professional help is better and less expensive than ever.

Search out people holding the CFP® credential or members of NAPFA (National Association of Personal Financial Advisors). Other designations or experienced professionals could be good, too, but they'll require added scrutiny.

How Bonds are Vital to a Successful Portfolio

Bond prices fluctuate differently than stocks. This is mostly because they pay regular interest to investors. So, no matter how the bond's price changes, the owner can expect that semi-annual pre-determined interest payment until the bond matures. Also, at maturity, the investor can expect to get a full payment for the principal amount.

These two factors are important. Most common stocks don't offer regular dividend payments or a guaranteed pay-off at some future date. This is one reason why some bit of news can alter a stock's price in minutes or seconds. Simply, there is no cash income stream to offset the uncertainty of stock ownership. Stock prices can fluctuate wildly at certain points.

With bonds, cash income helps offset bad news, but it doesn't necessarily eliminate fluctuations. Known income streams (cash interest and payment in full upon maturity) offer certainty, but they don't offer absolute certainty. Bonds can default and there is no assurance that a lengthy stream of payments will stay competitive over time. How is that 2% bond payment going to feel a few years from now when new bonds are paying 3%?

The Variables That Matter Most

Although daily prices fluctuate for all bonds, they are most dramatic with two variables. The longer a bond has until maturity, the more dramatic the fluctuations. That's because there is higher risk that the income stream may become uncompetitive or insufficient. Also, some bonds face a much higher prospect of default than others; a corporate bond issued by a troubled company will see more price volatility than a bond backed by the U.S. Government. A long-maturity bond offered by the U.S. Government will fluctuate more than a short-maturity one.

Rising interest rates are always bad for bonds, no matter how good they are rated by Moody's. It's simple math; if you own a 10-year government-backed bond today, it will pay 2% each year until 2026. But new bonds maturing in 2026 may pay higher rates! If so, you are stuck holding a 2% bond in a 3% environment. Anyone you try to sell it to will want a hefty discount. Longer bonds are worse, shorter bonds are better. None of that has anything to do with the rating, but low-rated bonds will do even worse in this kind of environment.

Bond ratings are important because they are an independent assessment of the issuer's financial situation. Rating agencies (Moody's is the best known) study a company's books and issue a bond grade based on financial stability. In the bond world, U.S. government-backed bonds are the gold standard for safety and carry a AAA rating. From there, bonds move down to AA, A, BBB, BB, and below. BB or above are considered "investment-grade." Although ratings can change – a good company gets hit with a major lawsuit, say – ratings don't usually change due to the daily news or current events. Most rating changes reflect a shift in the issuer's financial condition.

Choosing and Monitoring Bonds

So why would anyone ever buy a longer- or lower-rated bond? Because they pay higher interest! That's called reaching for yield and it works best when rates are stable or falling. In other words, pretty much the last 20+ years.

So, among bonds, there will always be some fluctuation in prices. But the amount of fluctuation can be controlled through deliberate choices about the actual bonds or sectors held. Similarly, they can be controlled through the bond maturity (computed by a statistic called duration in a bond portfolio). Within maturities or sectors, bond prices usually fluctuate within a range. That range (again, usually) is much smaller than a stock portfolio. Proper bond portfolio design requires the same deliberate process as stocks.

Most long-term portfolios feature both stocks and bonds and the design should be appropriate for each client's situation and objectives. It is important to remember that stocks and bonds each play a role for diversified portfolios, and that they "play well together." Often, they exhibit opposite responses to the same piece of news, but even if they go up or down together, their rates of change can be vastly different. For all these reasons, choose and monitor the bonds side of each portfolio, just as the stock side.

Bond Funds

For many investors, it makes sense to hire expertise for bond portfolios. It's so much more efficient – a few million dollars in bonds could easily be 100 or more individual bonds. With different ratings and maturities, that's a lot of moving parts for that portion of a portfolio. Plus, and this is quite important, volume matters a lot in the pricing and trading of bonds. A quality mutual fund or unit trust manager likely supervises billions in bonds; they monitor and trade for a mere fraction of the cost for retail investors. Also, quite important again, volume suggests expertise with bonds that can't be duplicated by amateurs. Much like stock portfolios, I often recommend several different managers for different segments of the bond markets.

Good bond managers won't have a crystal ball, but they will respond as needed within specified portfolio segments. Although the specter of rising interest rates has been with us for years, it's impossible to predict the timing or magnitude of changing rates. Rates will rise, but the when and how much are unknown.

Bonds are often neglected in investment portfolios. The main reason is that they are retained more for balance than return. Their primary role is to mitigate portfolio volatility from growth (stock) assets. Generally speaking, the more bonds, the less portfolio volatility. As ballast, their returns are less important than their stability.

Still, understanding how bonds work is one key to portfolio success. It's a mistake to ignore this vital segment of portfolio construction.

PERFORMANCE IS A BAD MEASURE OF VALUE

Sometimes, people apply mental mathematics in evaluating advisory fees.

"Let's see," they'll muse. "If I can get five percent by myself, and you charge one percent a year, then you'll have to get six percent or more for me to come out ahead."

This simple logic is not only counterproductive, it's dead wrong.

First, performance isn't the only measure that counts. If performance were all that mattered, then we'd all drive Porsches or Ferraris. Truthfully, we also care about safety, reliability, comfort, and cost. When considering all factors, we almost universally choose something different than the highest performance available.

So, mentally charging a professional fee against just one of these variables—performance — is a distortion of what you really want and also of what you should expect from a quality adviser.

Here's another way to think about it. Looking back, two separate portfolios earned eight percent last year. One was invested completely in the common stock of a single local company, the other in a diverse mix of blue chip stocks. Does it matter which one you own? From a pure performance standpoint alone, the answer probably is no (that year, anyway). But any solid adviser would tell you that the comfort, safety, and reasonable expectations from these two portfolios are dramatically different.

If an adviser makes your situation safer, more reliable, more comfortable, and/or less expensive, then he or she has provided something you didn't have before. He or she has added value, even if he or she didn't add "net" performance. Millions of very smart people understand that's worth paying for.

Sure, it's an added cost, but those are added benefits, too, and the value of each benefit isn't directly tied to performance. So, mentally, it's a terrible mistake to use performance as the only evaluation criterion.

There are other points, too. It's entirely possible that a good adviser will create additional performance, not by being smarter or by "figuring out" the market (a fool's game) but by suggesting newer products, lower fees, or ideas beyond your personal experience. The adviser may broaden your portfolio in ways you've never even considered. There's no guarantee, but most observers believe that, over reasonable time horizons, added expertise adds performance.

Another important factor is not so obvious. Risk is a key component of investing, and many individual investors don't have a clue. An adviser brings experience, knowledge, and risk measurement tools to each situation. This expertise may not seem important, but it's critically important during market turmoil. Again, it's added value apart from performance.

A good advisor has worked with hundreds of clients, many with circumstances like yours. They've seen what works, what doesn't, what offers the best odds for success. Those are valuable insights. Good performance is important, but it won't mean a thing unless you accomplish your family goals and objectives.

It amuses me when people think they can manage their own portfolios just as well as full-time, properly trained professionals—all in the name of saving money. Millions of smart, successful people gladly pay advisers for assistance. They don't have money to burn; simply, they perceive comprehensive value that overrides the fees paid.

Part 3

SOLID HELP CAN

KEEP YOU SANE AND

HAPPY

CLIENT VALUE AND THE BELL CURVE

President Harry Truman once complained that what he needed most was a one-armed economist because nearly all of them concluded suggestions with "on the other hand ..." before launching into an exactly opposite argument!

Name any idea or subject and there will be a full range of knowledge and opinions. Examples are endless; from the proper color for automobiles (black, white, and silver are the three most common) to complex economic theory.

For most things, there is a pattern to this diversity. Most observations clump around the middle, with outliers at the extremes. In science and academia, this is called Gaussian or normal distribution and it is illustrated with a bell-shaped curve. Normal distribution and the bell curve have been tested and apply to almost everything, from human height to test scores to the traffic speed on an interstate highway.

I'll leave math out here, except for this one fraction. Roughly two-thirds (2/3) of usual observations clump in the middle, with the other third (1/3) split between opposite extremes. Here's how it works: Most sources report that the average height for an adult American male is 5'10" with a standard deviation of around 2.9". In terms of normal distribution, this means that two-thirds (2/3) of American men are between 5'7" and 6'1" tall. The other one-third are either shorter than 5'7" or taller than 6'1".

Got it? Okay, so now let's make a leap to personal finance. What are factors that are most important to personal financial success? Let's pretend that some combination of financial knowledge, good behavior, and good fortune (luck) are responsible for most financial success. If we had a way to quantify each of those (or any other factors you might want to add), we could create a scale and measure them. And, again, guessing here, we might conclude that most people fall in the middle, while a few are extra good and a few extra bad. If a normal distribution occurs, just one-sixth (1/6) is awful and the other five-sixths (5/6) are better than that. Most people, of course, fall into that big clump in the middle.

I'll also guess a similar normal distribution for advisors. Most are decent, a few are great, and another few are terrible. You decide the specifics on factors and scale: I'd guess a combination of knowledge, people skills, empathy, and a client-friendly employer. You may throw in specific experience or personality traits or even height, I don't care. The point is, no matter how you finally measure it, professional advisors are likely to populate a bell curve.

All this brings me to a very interesting question. *How much good is the normal advisor for the normal person?* I'm thinking about the middle two-thirds of both groups. It seems to me that most people could use some help, and that most advisors could be helpful.

Professional help isn't free. There are brokerage, insurance, banks, mutual funds, accountants, and independent advisory firms. All employ charming people who would love to help. Confusingly, there is not a lot of uniformity in products or services they offer. Even worse, fee schemes range from reasonable to outrageous (probably on that same curve).

For an individual, the fee system can be almost random; dictated by who they ask to help and the provider channel. There is a retail/wholesale structure that operates in layers of commissions, transaction fees, and product expenses. Often, smaller purchases impose higher costs, while larger buyers can enjoy substantial discounts.

So, cost of help is an important element of the answer. Simply, does the value of professional help exceed the cost for most people? Sometimes products impose rigid and costly fees. If annual expense ratios on a mutual fund or unit trust is high, that works against any value the advisor might bring. If products impose sales commissions, too, it's going to be even harder to overcome that cost barrier.

A recent study by the Russell Investments organization entitled *The Value of a Fiduciary Advisor Reaches 4% in 2017* affirmed the ongoing value of a quality advisor. This study (fifth in an annual series) pegged the value of a Fiduciary Advisor at 4 percent each year. The research methodology determined 5 areas where advisors added value:

- Selecting investments (0.33%)
- Financial planning (0.75%)
- Tax planning (0.8%)
- Portfolio rebalancing (0.2%)
- Helping clients avoid behavioral mistakes (2%)

These are all important for investors. Some advisors are probably better suited for some of these areas, but this research included an important distinction: fiduciary advisors operate under a specific set of rules different from many other industry providers.

Although I have seen studies about fees, I've never seen the range of industry fees applied to a bell curve. Still, fiduciary or not, most industry fee schemes probably don't approach the 4% annual threshold. My considerable experience suggests that some of the worst may approach 4% annually, but the rest are lower than that.

From all this, *it seems to me that the normal fee from the normal advisor is likely a pretty good value for the normal client.* If I am right, clients are probably decently served as long as they avoid the worst fees from the worst advisors. That's my argument against the idea that "most" advisors are bad. Or, said another way, even decent advisors add value beyond the costs they impose.

But there's no mistake that bad apples taint the industry. That's true just like every other profession. It is worth a special mention here, though, simply because that bottom one-sixth (1/6) imposes overwhelming barriers. Unfortunately, clients, not advisors, bear those costs of failure. Having a great advisor is good but having a bad one is devastating.

SALES COMMISSIONS HURT INVESTMENT CUSTOMERS

Sales commissions are a spectacular management tool. They encourage and reward employees for desirable behaviors. For instance, bank employees might be paid an extra $10 for each new credit card application they collect, or waiters might earn an extra dollar or two for anyone ordering a daily special off the menu.

I learned about sales commissions in business school. Sales, marketing, and management courses taught the benefits of aligning company objectives with employee compensation. It's a win-win any time you can pay people directly from the proceeds of their work. The pay scheme focuses attention on the activities that directly impact company profits.

Salary is usually the highest cost for companies and commission pay flows to the people who create profits. If compensation is tied to profitable behavior or products, the highest producers will be the highest earners. Lower producers will earn much less money. In some businesses, lower producers earn nothing at all.

So, employees earn special incentives to help the company prosper. It's good business. Good for employees, good for profits, good for the company.

Maybe not so good for customers. In fact, few bank customers need another credit card and the diner's daily special is likely last night's leftovers. In truth, those incentives were heavily biased against the customer. The rewards were designed to benefit the company.

This paradox is even worse for customers in the investment industry. Here are some of the reasons why:

A sales commission raises the cost. No question, the cost of the commission is built into the product. Any mutual fund, partnership, or annuity paying a 5% sales commission costs you an extra 5%. You won't see it, but it will manifest in a lower yield or less favorable terms. That exact same product offered without commission ("no load") will save customers 5% either at the time or purchase or over the product's life.

A sales commission reduces flexibility. This is precisely why some investment products feature hefty and long-lived Surrender charges. That a way for the company to assure enough future profits to pay the salesperson up-front. But, again, a Surrender charge is never good for the customer. The same product, without a Surrender charge would be immensely better for almost any customer.

A sales commission limits your options. The investment world offers millions of different products. Today, Morningstar® tracks thousands of different mutual funds or different share classes. But a commissioned salesperson only earns pay from the sub-set that pays commissions. That is a severe limitation, especially since many non-commissioned funds ("no-load") feature lower costs or better ratings from Morningstar®.

A sales commission often bolsters proprietary products. A captive insurance agent only offers one company's annuities and products; a different agent with a different company offers different annuities and products. The customer never sees all the options, just what each person can sell. In the brokerage world, mutual funds or internally-manufactured products sometimes earn higher sales commissions.

A sales commission rewards the selling process, not the service process. We hear this a lot from new clients. "She was really great to help us buy that, but we never saw her again." Right. She was already off to the next paycheck. That's how the sales commission system works. In most cases, there aren't commissions for customer service.

A sales commission favors products that are hardest to sell, illiquid, or inferior in some way. Products that are easy to sell don't require commissions, or big ones anyway. There's a reason why annuities are so common today; many offer a sales commission of 5-8%. That might not sound high, but it could garner a $20,000 paycheck from a typical 401(k) Rollover. No wonder the salesperson is so charming!

A sales commission influences your advisor, and that influences recommendations. Salespeople usually dispute this, but business schools know it is true. I often explain that advisors want to do the best they can for customers within the framework of their own company and situation. But that framework includes training and sales materials. Salespeople know little about the other companies or products in the marketplace. They commonly think their products are the perfect solution to every problem.

Although sales commissions are still common, they are vestiges of a different era. That era stacked all the chips on the seller's side of the table. Every customer paid commissions because they didn't have a choice.

This new era offers thousands of good options without a sales commission, and better ways to pay for professional help if you need it. Sales commissions are a spectacular management tool. They are rarely, if ever, good for the customer.

WHY I HATE RELATIONSHIP MARKETING AND WHY YOU SHOULD, TOO

Relationship marketing is another paradox in finance and investing. The idea of rationality in financial decision-making has been abandoned by nearly everyone in recent years, partly in response to overwhelming evidence from the behavioral finance crowd.

Research shows that most people error in the ways they approach investing. They routinely overweight recent performance, favor recognizable company names, and re-live the trauma from market downturns. There are a host of other biases, but that's another column for a different day. Let's just leave it that most of us aren't as rational as we'd like to believe.

Today, I'm thinking about a different sort of irrationality. This is the (very human) desire to do business with people we already know and like. This is especially true for investing. I attribute this mainly to the challenge of finding trustworthy information in a world of disturbing noise. Television, radio, newspapers, magazines, and e-mail bombard consumers with countless financial messages and those messages are confusing and contradictory.

One way to sort through that noise and clutter is to find a good advisor for help. With the right advisor, you might tune out the noise and focus on more enjoyable pursuits. Money is important, but only as a tool towards other family goals. Let a competent expert focus on the money so you can focus on better things. It's a sound idea and I recommend this to people all the time.

People typically choose an advisor based on existing relationships. They choose someone they already know, or someone recommended by a friend, or someone they recognize through advertising. Sometimes, they'll take false comfort in big brand names or well-known buildings. They'll favor advisors who are popular, attractive, and charming. A psychologist could offer a reason for each of these, but that doesn't make them your best choice!

Top financial marketers understand these tendencies and use them to attract new business. Investing is a billions-dollar business and successful firms know exactly which buttons to push. Have you noticed how much advertising looks the same from company to company?

So, consumers often use relationship cues to find an advisor - and they aren't all that sound. Using cues is easy, but the challenge and solution is far more complicated than that.

Advisors come from various backgrounds. They enter the investment world through brokerage firms, insurance companies, mutual fund families, accounting firms, law firms, banks, and trust companies. The training they receive is specific to each industry and, in fact, each competing firm. Licensing exams are required for most advisors but passing a licensing exam is a very minimal requirement.

All this is to say that ability and knowledge is not universal or even particularly high. Passing a licensing exam allows you to work in the industry; yet, many successful exam takers won't survive beyond a year or two. The industry knows that a newbie agent or broker is more likely to fail than succeed. (Side note: don't immediately switch your investment accounts to help a newbie child or relative ... chances are high that they won't be there a few years from now.)

As marketers, each industry segment features a unique sales proposition and perspective. Insurance agents tend to tackle problems in a similar way, as do brokers or tax advisors. There may be merit to each different approach, but they are not equally good for your circumstances. Saving taxes isn't equally beneficial to all investors. A life insurance policy could be just the thing for a young family, but less desirable for retirees. One size doesn't fit all; one set of products can't serve all clients equally.

Relying on the usual relationship cues is a random approach to choosing an advisor. Relationship marketing doesn't address your needs or specifics or your situation. Choosing someone you like and know may mean choosing someone without necessary knowledge or skills.

The advisor you really need may not know you or your friends, and the firms spending millions on advertising are likely bigger, not necessarily better. A limited number of genuinely competent advisors are popular, attractive, and charming. The nerd from 5th grade may be a lot more competent than your class president!

Here's what I suggest to overcome the relationship cue bias:

- Seek out advisors who serve other clients like you. The best financial solutions will be tried and true for similar people.

- Research advisors on government sites and review their disciplinary history and employment record (https://www.adviser info.sec.gov/). Frequent job changes or blemishes are a red flag.

- Take special note of financial education and credentials. This can be confusing, but genuine credentials beyond licensing exams suggest some initiative and dedication.

- Choose advisors who are product-independent. Products are a tool for meeting your specific objectives, not a panacea for all clients.

- Seek someone who is both pleasant and forthright. Doctors are a good example of what you want; someone to tell you the truth and put you on a healthy path.

- Inquire about insurance protection against institutional failure, employee fraud, or professional negligence. If they stumble around discussing any of these, run for the exits.

- Understand all fees involved in hiring them. Ditto.

Oddly, experience alone is both over-rated and under-rated in advisors. Experience isn't a grand credential because much of the industry favors selling over expertise. There are a ton of top salespeople with lackluster knowledge or ability. On the other hand, a lot of valuable skill comes from direct contact with clients. The newest license in the shop rarely has a necessary foundation to hit the ground running. You don't want or need to be their guinea pig.

Don't be random in choosing an advisor. Yes, relationships are important. In choosing an advisor, you should look for someone with the necessary skills and knowledge to help you succeed. And you should plan on building a strong partnership in that effort. Done right, you will enjoy a meaningful, helpful, and friendly relationship. That's how professionals work, and that should be your goal in choosing an advisor to help.

UNDERSTANDING INVESTMENT FEES IS CRITICAL TO SUCCESS

Finally, fees have earned their rightful place as one factor in proper investing. The popular media, government regulators, and informed consumers are realizing just how important costs are to investment success. I applaud that general awareness, but there is still work ahead.

Investment fees can be insidious, and there is a reason for that. Warren Buffett once observed that a footnote to a financial statement was incomprehensible "for a reason." Similarly, investment management fees are often deliberately complex and obscure.

FEE PYRAMID

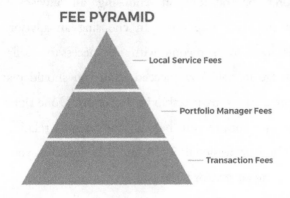

I created this Fee Triangle to simplify and highlight typical portfolio fees. Our strong belief is that transparency alone reduces fees. Shine a bright light into a room and roaches and other creepy creatures scurry for cover; the same is true of unfair or elevated pricing schemes. Just knowing where to shine that light will bring overall costs down!

Local Service Fees. The first layer of fees is the most obvious: local investment management fees. Your trust company or department, RIA, or asset-based manager charges these fees and it's usually a percentage of the portfolio size (Assets Under Management or AUM). For nonprofits, the typical competitive bid situation compares this cost between various vendors.

Portfolio Manager Fees. The second layer of fees is less obvious. These are third-party portfolio fees, and they are a component of mutual funds, hedge funds, exchange traded funds (ETFs), unit trusts, REITs, and other managed products. Morningstar® offers in-depth coverage of these fee ratios and costs. If your portfolio features Separate Managed Accounts – individual stocks or bonds managed by a third-party manager – those management fees are included in this tier, as well.

Tier 2 fees can be easily managed. The investment product marketplace features thousands of good choices. There is literally no reason to choose a high-priced product when there are hundreds of better-priced options. Pricing information on mutual funds, hedge funds. ETFs, unit trusts, REITs, and other managed products should be compared before using. If you can't find the cost for a product, seek another.

Transaction Fees. This third layer of fees is most insidious of all. These are transaction fees, and they are often hidden in the trades. So, if your portfolio buys a thousand shares of stock, it pays a commission on that trade to someone.

It will be reported on a confirmation, if you get one, but custodians might simply report the trade at "net" prices (after the trade costs).

There can be huge differences among the level of transaction fees charged to each client. Volume can and does make a difference, but few clients see these fees without asking. Still, because they aren't obvious, they can be significant.

Fees typically come in layers

Many traditional investment portfolios could have fees from all three layers, although some providers may feature just one or two. A stockbroker might recommend a stock or bond, and his payment would be through a transaction commission (Tier 3). If he or she recommends a mutual fund, there's a likely sales commission (Tier 3), plus ongoing fund manager fees (Tier 2). Buy a similar no-load fund direct from the fund family, and you'll just pay Tier 2 fees.

In some traditional pricing models, bargains in one tier may be promoted while profits are made through a different one. For instance, front-end loads on mutual funds (sales commissions) might be replaced by inflated and less obvious fund manager fee. With mutual funds, this is often accomplished through multiple share classes of the same fund.

As a Registered Investment Advisor (RIA), our usual approach with clients is to use No-Transaction-Fee (NTF) managed portfolios, and we charge a local AUM service fee. So, our typical client pays a local service fee (Tier 1) plus portfolio manager fees (Tier 2), but mostly without any transaction fees (Tier 3). Other RIAs might take a similar approach for their clients.

Importantly, it's the total fees that matter to performance, not the particular fee scheme (although a scheme may matter for conflict of interest or other reasons). Simply, most investment performance is tied to broad market averages, instead of individual stocks and bonds. The cumulative effect of layered fees directly impacts portfolio returns.

We see many instances where layered fees inflict a crushing blow to performance. The most offensive fees are often hidden in the darkness of Tier 3. These don't readily appear without knowledgeable and persistent persuasion. Still, shine some light on them and they'll likely get better. That's what fee transparency does for investors.

CHOOSING AN ASSETS UNDER MANAGEMENT (AUM) FIDUCIARY MODEL FOR YOUR PORTFOLIO

Fees are a huge part of investing. I'm always surprised when someone explains to me that they are paying "low fees" of "no fees" for investments. The roadway from Wall Street to Main Street is paved with fees and there is no way to avoid them entirely.

And, truthfully, most fees result from some added value. The firm that creates an investment deserves to be paid, just as the firm distributing it. Everyone gets paid and everyone deserves to be paid.

But that doesn't mean that every consumer needs every added service. An investor who does her own research probably doesn't need a full-service brokerage firm or the accompanying cost. It's wasteful and expensive to pay for services you don't need.

Sometimes people don't know what they need. And some very smart people choose to delegate investment services even though they could perform them themselves. One good choice under these scenarios is the so-called Assets Under Management (AUM) fee. Simply, you choose someone else to make investment decisions for you. If you do it right, that someone or institution has experience and expertise way beyond your own. The potential value can be enormous.

These arrangements are most common with investment advisory firms or trust companies, although some brokerage firms provide similar services. These programs can provide exceptional value if you understand what you are getting for your fee.

First, an AUM fee is not a mere portfolio management fee and should not be compared to a mutual fund or wrap fee. The Assets Under Management (AUM) model rises from a fiduciary standard. It's a stewardship model. It's not appropriate to compare it to other investment management because it involves a much higher standard.

A fiduciary is buying on your behalf:

A fiduciary – a Registered Investment Advisor or trust company – accepts *responsibility* for your portfolio. Both moral and legal responsibility. *They are accepting a requirement to act in your best interest and engage our professional knowledge, experience, and judgment on your behalf.* They employ detailed processes, procedures, and systems to design, implement, and evaluate your investments. They are not selling you a product or products. They are buying them on your behalf. It's a completely different paradigm.

An illustration of these points:

Imagine for a minute that you will accept this same kind of responsibility in caring for someone's home. They ask you to accept moral and legal responsibility for all their property and possessions (this concept of stewardship hails all the way back into Biblical times). They'll pay you a fair stipend each year for accepting this responsibility. Of course, you are also accepting some liability including their potential claims if you fail to perform responsibly. Let's say you agree to do this for $5,000 this year.

For that $5,000, you agree to arrange care and maintenance of their property. Lawn care, gardening, utility payments, taxes, insurance, and routine expenses. A tree falls, and you arrange for it to be removed. A window breaks, bats get in, and you call the exterminator and window repair company. The owner pays for these services, but you make sure they are done right, and that the property stays immaculate. And if one of the vendors fails to perform or steals a painting off the wall, both he and you might be sued! No worries, you think, I'll accept that risk for $5,000 per year.

So how much should you charge for the 500-acre estate down the street? Your duties and responsibilities are roughly the same, but the ramifications are so much larger. There's a swimming pool, farming operation, equipment, and employees. There's a security operation and 24/7 monitoring. And – this is important – the potential lawsuits are larger by a factor of 10 or 15 times!

In other words, *the larger estate commands a much bigger responsibility even if the duties are similar!* Even if they take a similar amount of time each week. It's not the time that matters, it's the amount of responsibility with additional specialized knowledge, experience, and judgment.

That difference is fiduciary responsibility:

That difference is fiduciary responsibility. The lawn service mowing both yards charges based on the size of the lawns. The agent selling insurance simply collects data and forwards it to the insurance company; he collects a premium and moves on. Those are project work, not ongoing responsibilities.

One argument against AUM fees is that complex/large clients could require more attention. An AUM fee *can be* unfair for the client and it *can be* unfair to the advisor. But it isn't necessarily unfair to either. Sometimes yes, sometimes no. My experience is that most times, a small account requires just as much attention as a larger one, but the larger one generates a lot more revenue. That's a generalization.

AUM fees acknowledge the responsibility involved in faithfully overseeing your investment portfolio. It's a complex service, but it is also an added value. A growing number of informed investors are choosing this comprehensive approach to investing. For them, and perhaps for you, an AUM fee represents good value.

FIVE QUESTIONS EVERYONE SHOULD ASK WHEN LOOKING FOR A FINANCIAL ADVISOR

I started in the trust department of a bank back in 1984. It was my lucky day because I've learned the investment business by helping successful people. It's a rich irony that successful people use quality advisors while others won't spend the money.

Jump to the end of this column if you want to know specific reasons an advisor makes such a big difference for so many people. For everyone else, I'm going to walk you through some ideas for finding a quality advisor and some questions to ask before choosing.

One of the toughest things about choosing an investment advisor or financial planner is narrowing the field of choices. Across most cities, there are hundreds of people working in insurance, brokerage, banking, or advisory firms. Nearly all of them want to help.

- All these people are licensed in some fashion. That's a government requirement to sell or advise about investment securities and it's usually the first step in a financial career. Passing a test is the bare minimum, though, and you should seek a higher standard for help.

- I also suggest college graduates with some sort of relevant degree. Graduate degrees are even better because they show determination beyond the norm. Show me a master's degree in business, accounting, or finance and I'll show you someone who went the extra learning mile.

No, an advanced degree isn't required, but it's proof of effort and ambition.

- Professional credentials are another step up. The Certified Financial Planner™ designation has become industry standard for personal finance. A few others – Chartered Financial Analyst and Certified Public Accountant, for instance - require a lot of education and work beyond a simple license. But beware, many "Fake" credentials are out there to confuse and entice you, more marketing than substance.

- What else do I recommend? Experience, but it needs to be relevant experience. I want to see work with other people facing similar challenges and opportunities as me.

From there, there are five basic questions everyone should ask before hiring an advisor:

How do you charge for services? Everybody gets paid. But you should understand exactly how your advisors will be paid for the work they do. No secret fees, no stumbling around answering this question. If they fumble or get defensive, keep looking.

What are your obligations to me? Any NAPFA® member or CFP® has a fiduciary duty to you (must put your interests above his or hers). Among others, the rules vary greatly. If the relationship is purely a selling\buying transaction, seek counsel before signing anything. I reviewed an article just last week explaining how certain insurance annuity salespeople aren't obligated to discuss other options that might meet your needs better or with less expense. That's a serious limitation.

What will you expect of me? It takes two to tango and a good relationship requires transparency, honesty, and willingness to learn. Every situation is different, but there are some basic principles in personal finance … if you won't follow them, you won't succeed.

What kind of people work with your firm? Every advisor worthy of your attention has worked with hundreds of people and seen a lot of situations. But it only matters if those people and situations are a bit like you. Advisors need to learn new stuff, but they don't need to learn from you.

What services do you provide? Similarly, not every advisor is good at every financial thing. Do you need tax preparation? Investment management? Budgeting or debt reduction? Welcome to the age of specialization.

Are you still wondering if you even need an advisor?

Many people reckon that professional advice costs money and they can save that much by helping themselves. But that thinking is often flawed, or at least short-sighted.

As I hinted above, there are widely accepted personal finance principles that tend to create success. You can read countless books or magazine articles that highlight these principles. It is not rocket science and almost anyone can learn them.

However, no two families are alike, and those differences often alter the formula for progress. This is precisely where a top advisor adds value. Since they've worked with many people, they recognize how your situation may differ from the norm and how to adjust for success.

This is also a powerful reason to ignore your friends and relatives: even if they look like you, they are not like you. Their income is different, their work histories are different, their children are different, their extended family is different. They'll need different resources in retirement and the things they need to do are different than the things you need to do. Seriously, most free advice is overpriced!

Bottom line? Most people don't know what they don't know. And not knowing can cost way more than the fees for a genuine professional. It's no coincidence that successful people have advisors.

THE CHOICE IS YOURS: ADVISOR OR NOT?

Did you ever think about who hires an advisor ... and why? I think many people assume that advisors are an unnecessary expense. They wrongly believe that knowledgeable people don't need one and that the only folks hiring advisors are rich or uninformed people.

Yet, that describes almost no one on our client list. Our clients are hardworking, smart, knowledgeable, and quite well-informed. Most of them spend wisely and few of them would pay for services they don't need. Indeed, most clients perceive value that we rarely see discussed in the press or media. Our list includes active businesspeople, teachers, professionals, union employees, and retirees.

Some writers drone on (and on and on) about fees, expenses, and performance. They seem to offer some credibility because they are – supposedly – unbiased. But that's just not so. They are biased, and here's their main bias: they want you to do-it-yourself. Seemingly, they won't be happy until every adult in America is scrolling CNBC and tweaking their investments daily. They preach the gospel of "long-term" while serving up a weekly (or daily) menu of urgent financial things to do.

Here's the huge point they miss. Part of what advisors offer to the marketplace is a *convenience* service. It's only marginally related to fees, expenses, and performance. People pay us to do things they'd rather not do themselves. And we also bring a level of expertise that they couldn't duplicate on their own.

Do you change the oil in your cars? Do you cook every meal at home? Do you grow all your own food and produce? Chances are high that you hire some of these things done and that the job they do is better than you'd do alone. I've enjoyed some remarkable restaurant meals and I promise the oil change guys are faster and better (and way cheaper) than me. Unless you just love changing oil, you know what I say is true.

Advisors have work because many savvy people don't want to do investments and finance! Not because they can't, or because they don't have enough information, or because they haven't seen any good articles about investing. Simply, they don't want to spend precious leisure time studying stock reports or mutual fund statements.

My wife and I recently moved to a townhouse. At our former home, we cut the lawn ourselves and trimmed the bushes, trees, and shrubs. We don't do that work anymore. We deliberately chose a housing option that reduced our workload. Now we visit with our children and grandchildren instead of working in the lawn. We are freed up from pesky chores and our evenings and weekends are open for the activities we enjoy.

Yes, we pay homeowner's dues and, yes, they might seem expensive or unnecessary to some people. A frivolous expense, perhaps, especially if you like doing maintenance or lawn work. *But it is worth every nickel to us.*

Should an advisor add performance or stability to your portfolios? Yes. Should they bring economies of scale to limit your total costs or add services beyond those you can perform yourself? Yes. Should they bring experience and expertise beyond what you can know on your own? Again, yes. Any advisor who doesn't do these things won't last long in the profession.

Here's what else advisors should do: they should free you up to focus on the things you really enjoy. They should provide easy-to-understand information so you can reach informed decisions. They should be around to take your phone calls or answer your email. They should be a knowledgeable and wise reference source for your specific circumstance and needs.

It takes a genuine professional to work towards the goals you want. And it is perfectly reasonable to say, "one of those goals is that I don't want to do this anymore."

There is an old story supposedly from Martin Luther King. A young man watched an older woman enter the city bus and start moving down the aisle towards the back. "Hey, didn't you hear that we don't have to sit in the back anymore? We marched and won our right to sit anywhere we want." She shoots him a glare. "I was marching right beside you. Now that we won, I want to sit in the back where there is more room for my packages."

Choosing not to do-it-yourself is just fine. That's a huge point often missed about money.

Just a small percentage of our population actively manages their own money. Still, though, they are a very small group. One knowledgeable source pegs them at just fifteen percent of the population. Here's my question. Who helps the other eighty-five percent? Are they really getting the help they need and want?

Part 4

TRULY HELPING

OTHERS MAKES US

HAPPY

AVOID THE GRIEF BOMB

Everyone encounters grief differently. There are stages of grief and some people linger over each stage. Others jump back and forth or skip stages or even miss them entirely. There's no normal and there's also no right or wrong.

There are a few universals, though. One universal is that everyone wants to help. No matter the circumstance or age or relationship, there's a strong desire to reach out. Family and friends bring food, flowers, condolences and expressions of faith, hope or remembrance. They pick up the phone or drop by or attend a celebration if there is one. They just want to do something.

And, of course, it's all appreciated. Family and friends are the only good remedy. Acts and words offer comfort.

Under this umbrella, though, I offer words of extreme caution. *Please resist the temptation to provide financial advice.*

We sometimes jump to this old standby when we can't bake cookies or write flowery sympathy cards. We want to help, so we go where we feel most comfortable ... talking about finance or investments.

I call this the grief bomb.

Take a powerfully emotional moment, toss in a few nuggets of homespun advice, stir in numbness, anger, agitation, and confusion. Along comes an authority figure or trusted friend (or mere acquaintance) with a financial suggestion or idea.

Boom! A bad situation just got worse.

Why? Because there is so much that friends, relatives, and colleagues don't know (I call these people FRCs, pronounced Freaks). They probably think they are helping. But bad advice, even with stellar intentions, often has disastrous consequences.

These are the correct versions of just a few topics that FRCs get wrong:

- Most common spousal transfers aren't taxable. For most couples, assets are held in joint ownership. The survivor gets the asset automatically upon death. No tax.

- Wills only apply for assets held in single name. No minor children? No assets in sole name? A will isn't necessary and doesn't apply.

- IRA, retirement accounts and pension payments transfer via Beneficiary Designation (only!). Surprisingly, a won't apply here, either. Whomever was designated beneficiary gets the money. Life insurance proceeds aren't taxable. People struggle with the notion that this large payment doesn't require income or estate taxes, but it usually doesn't. And again, whomever was designated as beneficiary gets the money tax-free.

- The highest household Social Security benefit continues. Social Security is confusing, but this is the general rule for spouses. (This is one reason why good choices need to be made when starting benefits.)

- Most estates don't require probate. Probate is only necessary when a decedent owned property in sole name. See above.

- Some debt survives the deceased. Check with a lawyer on this, but most credit cards, mortgages and bank loans are issued to joint owners. When one is gone, the other is still responsible for the debts.

Chances are high that you learned something from this list and that proves my point. People don't know all these things and offering financial advice without knowing can be a major mistake! Offer sympathy and empathy but leave money matters to competent advisors.

Here are the five financial steps I recommend to survivors in grief:

Survive and stabilize.

1. Take care of yourself. Few financial things are urgent upon a death. Make funeral arrangements and pay other immediate expenses. Pay pending utility bills or household

items. Ask a friend or relative for help on these matters if you need it.

2. Survey, consolidate and simplify. It takes time to find records and accounts. Both health and life insurance may require months. Pensions and Social Security, too. Combine similar accounts and corral financial assets to a few convenient providers.

3. Solve for a new beginning. This is important and it takes deliberation. Stay in the same house? Same city? Same job? Same church? Make no major financial decisions until you know. Ask a counselor or trusted pastor if you need help. A year or longer is fine for this step.

4. Fund your new lifestyle. This is tougher than it seems. But once you've solved #3, it's time to align money and goals. Find a quality advisor to help implement a solid plan.

5. Systemize ongoing review and adjustments. This is where people falter. The world is complex, and survivors often live a very long time. Plans put in place today – no matter how

good they are – will need adjusting later. Again, a quality advisor is key to long-term success.

Avoid the grief bomb. This is the wrong time to be casual about personal finances. People enduring grief are emotional and vulnerable. They need our acts and words and attention. They don't need bad advice.

BEWARE THE YAK YAK BOMB

This is a special challenge for executives.

Business executives can face unique challenges with personal finance. People around them assume they know about finance and investing simply because they know about business. Why is this a challenge? Because the opportunity to offer advice is almost irresistible.

I spend an hour every weekday at the local YMCA. I've been doing it for years, and I've heard almost everything that could be said in a locker room. Politics, sports, weather, relationships … seriously, the day-to-day yakking is endless.

One day another exerciser asked me about some investment. I don't remember the early part of our conversation, but I'll never forget the conclusion. "That's not for me because I quit investing in anything that won't make me at least 50% a year." I still see him occasionally, and I always wonder how that worked out.

Knowing business may not help.

I also read about economics and investing. Basically, two types of people study investing. Professional advisors - including some accountants, certain lawyers, or business executives - need to keep sharp and stay informed. Do-It-Yourself (DIY) investors form the other group. They read because they like all things financial; it's an addictive hobby and many of them stay well-informed.

Although awareness of stocks, bonds, personal finance, and economics may be similar among both these groups, there is one big difference: Professional advisors draw from wider experience. Typically, a DIYer knows his or her own experiences plus a few others. A seasoned advisor has worked with dozens (or hundreds) of clients and brings that encyclopedia along for perspective. Plus - and this is enormously important - an advisor really knows each client.

Sharing with others isn't always a good thing.

The worst DIY investors have an obnoxious desire to offer advice. *I call this the Yak Yak Bomb.* They decry any fee and argue – often loudly – that it's stupid to pay for financial guidance or help. They judge value based on their own perceptions and then apply that to everyone else. This may be a small group among DIYers, but they make a lot of noise.

They argue about articles, social media posts, and anywhere else they find an audience. There is a warped need to proclaim brilliance in front of others. Almost any legit finance column faces angry retorts from these self-righteous experts.

Yakking is part of their fun. They brag about their conquests. They pontificate about the perils of recession (the perils of almost anything, actually). They opine about stocks or funds or gold bullion, maybe. They offer advice – strongly worded advice – to friends, relatives, and strangers in the locker room, kitchen, or office.

The Yak Yak Bomb can be dangerous.

This can be particularly harmful to an executive's colleagues and friends. Why? Because they are authority figures. If our boss or father offers a suggestion, we tend to follow it *even if it is not-so-good.*

Without broad perspective and a deep dive into personal circumstances, stand-alone knowledge is flawed. I've seen cases where a surgeon casually mentions some investment and people in the office scramble to buy it. Why? They liked him, they trusted him, and they (perhaps wrongly) recognized his financial expertise.

Even if that investment idea was sound, there's a big gap between the surgeon's circumstance and his office helpers.

Even among doctors themselves, the differences between one family and another can be profound.

I cringe every time I hear amateurs offer advice. The role of genuine investment and financial advising is highly regulated and requires study, testing, and – dare I say it – both people skills and situational knowledge. Experience helps, too.

Here's my bit of professional advice:

Warren Buffett has been quoted suggesting that investors buy an index fund or seek professional advice when they need it. He is widely recognized as one of the top investors in the world – and he knows when to refer out. Warren doesn't launch Yak Yak bombs, and neither should anyone else.

Honestly, most people don't share strong interest in personal finance or investing. They won't read articles or think endlessly about stock market antics. In fact, money tends to be a back burner issue in most households ... invisible or ignored until it bubbles over or causes some other disaster.

If someone asks you for help, refer them to a professional. Advisors can provide unique value in those situations. They step way beyond DIYers, or Vanguard or Schwab self-help, or other distant providers, and they do it for a very reasonable cost. That's reasonable defined by client and advisor, not as defined by well-meaning amateurs.

Each consumer gets to decide value based on their own needs and circumstances. Please let them.

HELP YOUR BEST EMPLOYEES SUCCEED FINANCIALLY

If you own or manage a company, you are a role model. Some role models are good, some are bad, but you are kidding yourself if you think people aren't watching your every move. If you are smart, you'll use this fact to help employees succeed financially.

Nowhere is this more important than personal finance. If our boss or father or other authority figure offers a financial suggestion, we tend to follow it *even if it is not-so-helpful.* I've seen cases where a surgeon casually mentions some investment or fund and people in the office scramble to buy it. Why? They liked him, they trusted him, and they (perhaps wrongly) recognized his financial ability.

Even if that investment idea was sound, there's a big gap between the surgeon's circumstance and his office helpers. Even among doctors themselves, the differences between one family and another can be profound. What seems good for one might not be best for another.

Don't be a bad role model.

I encounter smart bosses every day who have experience and opinions about finance and investing. Some of them are as knowledgeable about stocks, bonds, and economics as members of my own professional team.

What they lack, though, is perspective. They've read articles, studied budgets, browsed the internet, talked with a few friends and family. All good, but sort of isolated in a small bubble of similar situations, time horizons, and ideas. If your knowledge base rises from just these past ten years, that's a serious limitation on your ability. And it is a serious limitation on guidance you offer others.

Suggesting a seasoned professional is one way to offset limitations.

Simply, any competent advisor worth consulting has worked with hundreds of clients, diverse needs, and widely-varied economic climates. No guarantees, but the perspective offered is necessarily broader than your own.

There's one old (powerful) idea that helps makes this point. It's very common to hear that you should reduce or eliminate portfolio risk as you near retirement or when your portfolio is large enough to meet your needs. Or, as they say in football, take a knee when you've already won the game. This idea sounds great and, since many people are risk-adverse anyway, it encourages them to do what they already want (that's the easiest sell in any endeavor!).

But it might not be what is best. I don't recommend that anyone liquidate a long-term portfolio and take a knee. My professional recommendation would be to reduce risk assets, perhaps, but maintain a modest portion as an inflation hedge and for a few other reasons.

Many advisors recommend 25-35 percent in longer-term (5+ years) portfolios. Liquidity needs and potential taxes must be considered, too, and they differ from family to family.

This very common notion of eliminating risk requires more thought today and offers insight into how outside advice can help.

Retirement time horizons often run longer than people predict. So, the guy contemplating retirement at age 60 might assume that his $1 million 401(k) plan is enough for retirement. He's likely not thinking that he'll need income for 30+ years. A conservative, balanced portfolio might draw an inflation-indexed $40,000 per year for life. Shift it to bank certificates or money market funds and he'll gradually lose ground from year-to-year. The problem is less severe for someone at age 80, but it could still be a factor over another 15 years.

Another point is that market risks are less than they seem for periods longer than 5 years. While anything might happen during the next 5 years, the 5-year investment outcome is more predictable than people think. So, most times, people with 5+ years in their investment horizon will do better than they fear. Importantly, many people at age 80 or 85 still have a time horizon of 5+ years.

Third, even a small amount of portfolio "risk" adds significant compound returns. It's one thing to say, "we don't need any more money," but possibly another to deprive others. Heirs, charities, and other causes will gladly accept more when that day comes. Another way of saying this is that those parties might receive a gift diminished by inflation if you are too conservative with investing.

Comfort is important and every retirement portfolio should be carefully calibrated to an appropriate risk level.

Yes, too little risk can be as damaging as too much. With longer lives, broader perspective, and better understanding, many old ideas require new attention. The notion of eliminating portfolio risks in retirement sounds good, feels good, and may garner praise from some of your friends and family. *But that doesn't make it right.*

This isn't meant to disparage the fundamental idea of adjusting risk in your golden years. These are nuances to be considered as you think about retirement investing or discuss with others. And they are likely nuances that rise from outside your personal knowledge bubble.

As a role model, one of the best things you can do is model good personal finances with your own family. Another is to recommend professional help to your best employees and friends.

Part 5

RANDOM IDEAS FOR

HAPPY RESULTS

GOVERNMENT ISN'T A BUSINESS ...

Our founding fathers showed genuine genius in some of the things they created. Collectively, they envisioned a political system with both flexibility and resilience; our citizens enjoy so much as a result of their political and practical foresight.

Though brilliant, they missed on one interesting aspect of life today. In all their foresight, they never envisioned, they couldn't envision, two million federal government workers.

And that doesn't even include Postal service workers! By any account, government today has grown to be a big business.

Though big government isn't exactly a business, that doesn't mean it shouldn't run like one. In fact, management tools chosen to make profits on Main Street can be readily applied to accomplish other government goals.

If a business negotiates a better contract for office supplies, the amount saved could boost profits or it could buy better factory equipment. Likewise, savings in federal office supplies could serve more people in need, reduce government spending (and taxing), or even boost pay for deserving workers.

In business, the quest of profits is really a quest for efficiency. Good managers seek the best use of resources; it's a delicate balancing act of labor, money, knowledge, and materials. The right business mix results in profits for shareholders. The wrong mix results in losses or bankruptcy. An ongoing profit motive drives continual adjustments to the mix.

Profits provide an easy measure for this continual shuffling of resources. The mix is right when profits are high. The mix is wrong when they aren't. Professional managers have a large cabinet full of tools to measure, analyze, design, and implement a business plan. Some managers and teams are better at this than others; bad ones are fired, and good ones are highly-valued. New good and bad managers enter the work force each day.

Government should also seek continual adjustments to the resource mix. Citizens change all the time. Technology gets better, our knowledge base grows, employees gain experience, children grow up, tax revenues rise and fall. The right mix of labor, money, knowledge, and materials isn't the same today as it was ten years ago.

Similarly, good government programs today likely aren't the same as ten years back. In business, aging products or services are improved or removed. They are replaced by something better, or – if fewer people are buying them – they might be eliminated completely. Again, the quest for profits means that some competitor will offer a better product if you don't.

If profits aren't the right measure for government, what is? Well, that varies from program to program, but a meaningful measure is always there. If the goal is to feed the hungry, is that being done? How many people? Is the food nutritious? How much labor, money, knowledge, and materials are being used to meet that goal?

More importantly, can more (people, nutrition, quality) be done with a different mix of resources? Could we spend less money by beefing up technology or staff training? Could food contracts be re-negotiated? Could a different management team get better results with the same or reduced resources? These are common business challenges and there are credible tools to address them. Business schools throughout the country teach the principles. Good management is accepted science. The principles are universal. Simply choose the right goals and continually measure the outcomes. Adjust as necessary. Repeat.

Everything from poverty programs to health care to public education could benefit from decent business applications. Yes, there are already government programs in place today. Yes, they are staffed with "experts" claiming specific technical and sector knowledge. Yes, some of those programs have served the public well in the past.

But that simply isn't good enough. Could more be done with a different mix of resources? Could we spend less money by beefing up technology or staff training? Could contracts be re-negotiated? Could a different management team get better results with the same resources? Government isn't a business, but that doesn't mean it shouldn't run like one.

Our founding fathers created a wondrous political framework. But the business of government could still use some work.

Serving Nonprofits: Finance by Committee is Dangerous.

Many of us serve on charitable or nonprofit boards. It's a community role expected of business owners and executives. And, if you are like me, service seems to gravitate towards the finance committees. I'm often joined at the table by other executives, bankers, accountants, and probably a staffer or two. This seems like a good practice … but it's not.

Let's start with an analogy. Say your company car has 85,000 miles on it and it's time to choose a new one. You are pretty careful about the company's money, but you also enjoy a new car every few years and picking it out is half the fun.

New company policy: In order to engage with the customers, home office has declared that all new cars must be chosen by a group of your best customers. That group has been chosen by your boss and includes a grocery store manager, a local banker, the Ford dealer, and an art instructor from the neighborhood community college. There's also a business reporter from the daily newspaper.

Chances are good that everyone in this group has purchased a car before. In fact, you glance around the parking lot a few minutes before the first car selection committee meeting begins. Members arrived in a battered pick-up truck, a brand-new Ford, a late model import, and a Honda motorcycle. This ought to be really interesting!

Well, you get the point. No matter how well-intentioned this group, it's unlikely that you will end up with exactly what you want. And there's a fair chance that you'll get something powerfully different than what you want! Truthfully, you might be driving anything from a green hybrid SUV to a Greyhound bus by this time next month …

Investing by committee is similarly dangerous.

Committee members often have personal investment experience, and many of them work someplace in the finance world. They certainly have good intentions, but that's not always enough to make good choices. In fact, many of those characteristics actually cloud good judgment.

In making finance or investment decisions, nonprofits should seek safety, competence, convenience, and value. Portfolio composition should be a function of both monetary purpose and legal guidelines (*Uniform Prudent Investor Act* and the *Uniform Prudent Management of Institutional Funds Act*). All these things are verifiable and the matrix for evaluating these issues isn't burdensome or obscure. The science is straightforward.

Unfortunately, that's not how committees work. Any committee process is a complex web of psychology, sociology, power, and false illusions. There are always conflicts of interest, both subtle and not. And there's a mish-mash of both personal and institutional risk tolerances. What could go wrong?

Nearly everything. Especially volunteers without specific *institutional* portfolio expertise or history. Instead of focusing on fiduciary duties, or specific legal guidance, or even the advice from a reputable consultant, they choose heuristics (shortcuts) to make the job easier. It becomes a popularity contest of sizzle, flattery, community influence, and ill-perceived values. And the investment managers or other professionals vying for attention know all this. The sales process carefully embraces every group weakness.

So, it's not surprising when board members behave that way. It still bothers me, though. The fiduciary standard for nonprofit board members should weigh quality investment processes much higher than non-investment factors. Investing isn't a commodity product, especially with large portfolios … but, still, the worst reasons often win.

There's a little-known provision of both the Missouri and Kansas Prudent Investor Act that proclaims anyone who has special skills or expertise or is chosen in reliance upon special skills or expertise, "has the duty to use those special skills or expertise." In simple terms, if you're on the finance committee because you work for a bank or broker, you'd better do a quality job! *Your legal duty is higher than those around you.*

Again, the rules are straightforward. Hiring an investment, accounting, or banking firm simply because they've "been good to your nonprofit" isn't a prudent choice. There's more research required, and you likely have a legal responsibility to do it.

I remember this story from my youth.

A friend was explaining how angry he was over his experience in a basketball league. My friend was a talented player and practiced hard all the time. He did what the coach demanded and earned his coveted spot on the roster. Day in and day out, he was a quality basketball player. But it still irked him that another guy on the bench displayed far less talent and gave half-hearted effort at both practices and in games. That guy cost the team wins.

"I don't get it," I said. "Then how'd he get on the team?"

"Easy," my friend explained. "His daddy bought the uniforms."

GUERILLA SURVIVAL FOR NONPROFIT GROUPS

I've spent incredible energy with nonprofit groups. I've worked as a professional fiduciary since 1983 and my investment advisory firm today manages millions for charitable clients. I've waded through armies of nonprofit budgets and saved a few troubled groups from danger.

I once negotiated a settlement with the IRS for a large group that skipped withholding taxes for employee payrolls. In all, I've probably served on twenty different charitable boards and I've led several through treacherous financial minefields. Money is always short, and there is no scarcity of need in our society. But there are some things we can do to fortify our favorite organizations. These six financial strategies I suggest for guerilla survival in the nonprofit trenches:

Aim for the target – Nonprofit objectives seem clear, but they easily clutter. Keep focused on the mission. Tangents cost a lot of money and they often fail. Groups sometimes adopt tangential ideas that seem to offer revenue or influence. That's usually a mistake. Make sure every action moves you closer to the direct target.

Guard the provisions – Resources – money, time, and staff - are extremely precious among charities. Keep a watchful eye on budgets, expenses, and new programs. You must watch every single item every single month because it's almost impossible to take back lost ground when margins are so tight. The storeroom, human resources, and bank accounts require careful and critical attention. My wife served on a governmental board where millions were misappropriated over two decades; a clean audit was provided every year. Trust, but verify.

Screen for traitors and spies – Boards are usually comprised of well-meaning people. Yet, each has an agenda for participation. Some are much nobler than others. Vigilantly watch for conflicts of interest because they place the mission in peril. Corporate donors or board members are especially perplexing … carefully assess the cost/benefit of all relationships. Many times, intentions are good, but results are troubling. Money is not an end unto itself, money is a tool for accomplishing mission.

Monitor the Colonel – In the military, everyone is accountable to someone else. Not so in the nonprofit world where boards rarely fulfill their complete obligation to supervise and direct top management. Routinely meet without paid staff in the room because, sadly, absolute power can (and sometimes does) corrupt good people. In most cases, the board is charged with planning, training supervising, financial oversight, and stewardship of all resources. Management is charged with implementation. If the mission is struggling, the board needs to act.

Listen to the troops – One toll of leadership is isolation. Top managers and board members rarely hear the whole truth without digging. Solicit direct dialogue with people who actually deliver services. They know their business from doing it. They understand the finances because they see the direct results in action. Listen. I mean, <u>really</u> listen to their ideas and complaints. Ignore the strong tendency to keep financial discussions in the board room.

Abandon the dead – Don't pour resources into dying programs. Resources are precious and there is an opportunity cost for every expenditure. Money channeled to one program is not available for another. Proper allocation of resources is today's most critical job for most nonprofits. Kick unnecessary sentiment out of the boardroom. Make tough programming decisions before they become crisis situations.

This may seem like harsh language, but many nonprofits face a tough battleground today. In most cases, the nonprofit mission is more important than ever. The robust organization balances good intentions with smart financial sense. Tough decisions and dogged oversight are necessary practices for ongoing success. The best prepared army wins the war.

BEZOS ON MEETINGS: LEARN FROM A MASTER

I've admired Jeff Bezos of Amazon for some time. I'm an introvert and a reader, and my six decades have been enhanced by tens of thousands of books. I checked the other day and I've been an Amazon customer since 1998.

That love isn't universal, and I can see the perils of on-line merchandising. Still, as an entrepreneur and passionate capitalist, that business model is lightning in a bottle. Nothing since Microsoft DOS has grown so widespread or successful.

Bezos, like Gates before him, saw something no one else saw. But that is not enough. Great ideas are plentiful. Primo execution is rare. Taking a great idea from vapor to appliances delivered to my automobile trunk is brilliant, squared. Exquisite execution.

So, when I recently ran across Jeff Bezos' structure for running meetings, I stopped cold. My 40 years of business experience suggests that most meetings are wasteful, and most outcomes are mediocre. I choose that word carefully because mediocrity is the most common outcome for anything.

Simplicity is part of the solution. Bezos created a 3-rule Amazon structure for meetings. It is simple, but powerful:

- **Two Pizza Rule** – Smaller groups are better than larger groups.
- **Detailed Memo Rule** – Good decisions require a depth of information.
- **Study Hall Rule** – Everyone starts with the same information.

A traditional committee is a web of psychology, sociology, power, and false assumptions. And there's a mish-mash of both personal and institutional bias. It often becomes a popularity contest of sizzle, flattery, influence, and seat-of-the-pants ideas. Management decisions tend towards randomness or (even worse) predictability.

Detailed Memo Rule: Bezos' new structure combats uninformed opinions and wasted time. The structure's focus is a detailed memo: Bezos describes this as a six-page document with real sentences, verbs, and nouns. No bullets or Power Points. Writing the memo can take weeks, but that memo establishes a base-line knowledge for discussion. It also eliminates the often-false assumption that everyone has prepared for the meeting in advance.

Study Hall Rule: Great, you say. Who has time to write or read a long memo? Well, the author gets several weeks to craft and re-write, but reading it goes so much easier. "We read those memos, silently, during the meeting," says Bezos. "It's like study hall."

The eloquence of this is informed decision-making. The usual collection of mixed thoughts, ideas, and opinions is replaced by bona fide information considered by caring colleagues offering genuine perspectives. What a refreshing new idea! And the foundation for that meaningful discussion is built right into the process.

Two Pizza Rule: A committee is transformed into a small panel of experts. According to Bezos, no meeting should include more people than can be fed with two pizzas.

Did I mention execution? The heart of good execution is decision-making. The brain is solid information. The soul is caring people. His structure is a process that brings them all into sharp, reliable, and repeatable focus. Businesses execute plans every day. Darn few of them are as successful as Amazon. I'm listening.

How to apply this in our businesses? More deliberate depth is required for both customer and internal meetings. Start by including (just) the right people. Then:

- *Apply the structure where genuine collaboration can add value.* Many meetings are wasteful, but the notion of collective wisdom has merit. To be meaningful, though, crucial meetings must dive deep to banish the destructive biases, territories, and opinions that breed mediocrity.

- *Work from the same baseline.* Every customer or staffer walks in the door with a lifetime of experiences. They believe today exactly what those experiences have taught them. Create some sort of foundational memo to update and inform.

- *Teach and learn from informed sources.* One challenging legacy in my investment advisory business is a sales culture. This means that much commonly-accepted investment information is tainted by special interests. Clients and advisors suffer from this and one meeting objective is to provide deep and honest information to overcome these maladies.

- *Give important decisions the time they deserve.* The time to write a meaningful memo and the time to learn from it are both productive use of resources. But they aren't accidental; providing enough background information requires deliberate effort.

- *Change the collaborative focus from talk to execution.* It doesn't take much energy to be mediocre. Businesses do that all the time. But to be exceptional requires deeper understanding, energy, and a different approach. It requires a new way to think and a new way to act.

How you share this deliberately-deeper information in a meeting is up to you. Bezos advocates silent reading, but that likely works better for business meetings than customers. Still, it's certainly worth some extra time to create a common knowledge base with customers. Maybe a detailed summary of pertinent information?

The potential pay-off is in positive results. There's no promise of Amazon-like results – in fact, that would be nearly impossible – but that doesn't impair the process. Better outcomes should be the goal and the result for every meeting.

Most of us love helping people and running our business. We love the quest to get better. We love being inspired and inspiring others. Now, let's see what happens when we apply this powerful lesson from a true entrepreneurial master.

Part 6

CRISIS AND

TURMOIL CAN BE

GOOD

MY BUMPY PATH TO FINANCIAL HAPPINESS

*We caught Dan Danford in a contemplative
moment and asked about how turmoil has shaped
his life and career. It's a subject ripe for discussion
today, but he surprised us with both solid examples*

*and colorful stories. Maybe success isn't an accident
if you find the powerful lessons from each setback or
opportunity.*

**Amid the Coronavirus pandemic, we hear a lot of bad
news including doom and gloom about recovery from this
crisis.**

It's scary and troubling, no doubt. But crises and turmoil
have been good for me. My first 18 months in 1984 and 1985
were in the trust department of a failing bank. First Midwest
Bancorp was a holding company based in Missouri and they
didn't survive the national agricultural crisis. My stint as a
trust officer started in April 1984 – that same week they
reported large operating losses for the first time in a long and
storied history! Little did I know when I signed on ...

But today's crisis can be good for business? C'mon ...

It can be. First and foremost, businesses exist to serve
customers. And any crisis is a chance to grow and learn.
Customers may not even know what they need in a crisis, but
it's a good chance to show them. A crisis is an opportunity
and you can rise to meet it or let it defeat you. Do a good job
for people and they'll appreciate you forever. Today, we are
frantically re-balancing portfolios for clients ... they may not
understand the complexities of it all, but they see we are

working for them while much of the world is at a stand-still. Clients appreciate that and they'll remember.

And you claim turmoil and chaos was good for your career?

Several different times, actually. It wasn't always obvious in the moment, but I learned powerful lessons about client service and leadership. This was good-sized organization with affiliated banks throughout the region. It was instructional to watch the executive suite as they tried to calm nervous customers, placate employees, and satisfy shareholders. And, of course, many colleagues were all three! The top guys – they were all guys at that time – sang and danced with the enthusiasm of a burlesque circus. Sometimes the honesty and integrity were about that level, too.

So, what finally happened?

One October Friday, hundreds of government employees converged on the bank and branch locations and closed everything down. They were like ants, pouring in every door. It was all very dramatic, and we had to stay well into the night. Eventually, we were sent home with instructions to attend a Saturday morning meeting. There, in hushed tones, they announced Commerce Bank as our new bosses. Over the next year or so, a lot of top management and many former colleagues were fired or left. I was lucky enough to keep my job as trust officer, but mainly because I wasn't there long enough to screw anything up and my pay grade was low.

But you are better now because you were there then?

Of course. I watched one large bank implode from the inside, then learned a whole new system under another bank. It was like a crash course in the banking industry. I learned from some fine mentors and watched some incoherent fools. You either learned or died. It's also worth noting that this was the mid-1980s and the world was changing fast in other realms. The Federal government updated all the rules for pension and retirement plans and that boosted my personal stock again; suddenly, I knew as much as the people who had been working the field for decades. It was a rare growth opportunity for a smart young trust officer. Growth from chaos.

I'm guessing your story doesn't end there.

Nope. If a failing bank gave me a valuable start, a brand new one launched the next phase. After a few years, several of us in that trust department grew disillusioned with our new bank bosses. They weren't bad, they just weren't very good. We felt we'd done better before they came along – heck, we had nothing to do with agricultural lending – and they didn't show much regard for us or our trust clients. We decided we probably needed to leave.

So, this would be, what, 1987 or '88? Did you start looking around for a job?

Oddly, I turned down at least two good jobs around this time. But I was excited that we were considering change. I get bored sometimes and feel better if I can mix things up every so often! In this case, we approached the Commerce Bank board with an offer to buy the trust department for a sizable price. We reasoned that we ran it before them and they didn't seem very interested, anyway, so maybe they'd sell it to us? It was the right thing for us to do, but banking egos are huge. They looked at our offer as a criticism ... sure, in a way I guess it was, but they didn't have to view it like that. We should have known they would, though.

Bankers aren't always good with criticism.

That board sure wasn't. Talk about your turmoil. We had four key employees involved on our side and they fired the top one that very day. He called me from a downstairs phone in virtual shock. He was way more surprised than I was at the time! Over the next three days, all four of us were fired or quit, although they asked me to stay. Offered to make me a vice president and give me a nice raise, but, you know, I thought I deserved that long before they offered. I said, "no thanks" and went home to my wife and daughters.

Anyway, we immediately contacted the Missouri State Commissioner of Finance and enquired about chartering a spanking new trust company. This is technically a bank, but only offering trust and fiduciary services. No checking, savings, or lending products. No tellers or self-important branch managers.

Due to our urgency to feed 4 families, the new charter was granted in record time and The Trust Company of St. Joseph opened for business that January. Many of our clients followed in short order, and the independent trust company was an immediate success. We were profitable in our first year.

That's rare for any start-up. Why do you think?

Our history was very unique for one thing. The four of us had been together through a bank failure, a new owner, and now, the start of a brand new trust company. And our clients had been through it all with us. They were loyal and we were loyal, that makes some sense, right? None of this surprised me, but it surprised the hell out of other bankers in the community. Let me tell you, they put targets on our backs ... some of those targets are still there today, thirty years later. But their animosity spurred me on and created another reason to get up each morning.

Another glass of lemonade from a basket of lemons, right? The Trust Company rises from your dissatisfaction with the Commerce organization?

Yes, that's true. But two things really grew in me over this next ten-year period. First, my love for marketing. My college degree was business administration/marketing and I loved all aspects of promotion, advertising, and product development. The Trust Company was a clean slate and I had a blast. Everything from signage on the building to newsletters to coaxing news coverage from local reporters. We were remarkedly successful telling our story and it wasn't long before we had established a national reputation. I can't take full credit for it all but my personal marketing savvy was way beyond local norms. Our eventual growth far exceeded anything we – or our competitors – expected. We were smart and we treated clients well.

And the other passion that grew from this venture?

Entrepreneurship. I loved building that company. Weirdly, some of my colleagues weren't all that entrepreneurial. I mean, we started the company and it was successful, but they were more managers than entrepreneurs. Their involvement rose from circumstances instead of the passion that drives most genuine start-ups. But I loved it! I loved the challenges, I loved the competition, I loved the opportunity to guide our own ship and prosper through our own labors. I loved it then and I still love it today. Those years from the late eighties to the late nineties were some of the best of my career. We helped start the Association of Independent Trust Companies (AITCo) in Chicago and I served on the board. So much fun to meet and work with other professionals across the nation.

But you eventually left the Trust Company, too. What happened?

Well, it just became time for me move on. I was the youngster of the group – I was 42 in 1998 when I left – and the others were 10-15 years older. That meant I was 32 when we started, and I was starved for cash. Despite assurances about future ownership and compensation, they never came through in a way I felt was fair. The company became valuable faster than we expected and then they weren't so keen to share. But another issue was even more important to me. The entrepreneurial glow had faded … it was managers who owned the company and they didn't embrace opportunities I could see coming. This frustrated the hell out of me, and they just didn't get it at all. As I said, it was just time for me to move on. I walked out that door with nothing but an idea. No capital, no clients, no ties to a bigger organization. But it was a very good idea.

Family Investment Center?

Right. This was 1998 and the tech boom threatened traditional business models everywhere. Brokers and fund companies were evolving at record pace. The Internet was coming on fast and mobile phones were gaining broad usage. A brave new world was exploding around us and I believed strongly that investors would embrace new investment services and products. I had personally opened accounts with the Charles Schwab organization, and I loved the service package. I could write checks, use a debit card, transfer money remotely, invest with low or no commissions, and gather information about my money 24 hours each day. None of this was available through our trust company or most banks at that time. They were well behind the tech curve.

So, you called Chuck Schwab, right, and things grew from there?

No. Although he is one of my entrepreneurial heroes, I didn't meet him until years later. But his team in San Francisco build a powerful platform we adopted immediately for Family Investment Company. Legally, we created an independent Registered Investment Advisory firm to manage portfolios for clients. The firm was regulated under federal law and required that advisors serve as fiduciaries and earn fees, not sales commissions, from clients. For convenience and safety, the accounts had to be held at a third-party custodian – Schwab, in our case. It was a bold idea at the time, and it's grown to be a big chunk of the investment industry today. I didn't create the idea, but I was an early adopter. Maybe light years early for our local marketplace.

But you put your own stamp on it, right?

Oh, yes. I wrote a weekly newsletter called Table Talk and we mailed 40,000 of them to prospects in the early years. My teen daughters folded and stuffed the newsletters and I hand-signed every one of them. Forty thousand signatures in those first few years! As the business grew, it became impossible to keep that up, so our communications changed over time. But marketing and communications were the skills that set me apart. Did I mention that it was just me? It was a while before I hired any outside help but that didn't slow our early growth. We leveraged technology to do the heavy lifting.

You are independent.

We are a locally-owned corporation with shares owned by my family and several employees. We are genuinely independent, and we decide on all services, products, communications, and marketing. Though we work with Schwab and others to serve our clients, we do not pay them, and they do not pay us. Every nickel of revenue comes from client fees. We do a good job and get paid, or we don't, and we lose that revenue. Serve clients or die.

And that's grown to what today?

We proudly provide investment management and financial planning to hundreds of clients around the nation – and in other parts of the world. We have offices in St. Joseph – where we started – and Lenexa, Kansas, which is part of the Kansas City metropolitan area. Several of us are nationally-known in the advisory or planning profession and our names hit the national media regularly. The depth of our product and service package is unparalleled, from tax preparation to portfolio management and other scheduled financial planning activities.

Here's the thing. None of this would exist except for my experiences. And in a decades-long career, two or three crises taught me valuable lessons and prompted me into beneficial actions. Those were pivotal events and they created a lot of turmoil for me and others. But they also planted remarkable seeds of opportunity. I suspect today is the same.

CPSIA information can be obtained
at www.ICGtesting.com
Printed in the USA
JSHW052231200920
8024JS00002B/3

9 781506 909479